QUIET ASSURANCE

Meditations on Peace
for the Grieving Heart

THELMA NIENHUIS

Josh & Leah.

May you know the goodness
of God in both your grief
and your joy.

Thelma Nienhuis

www.thelmanienhuis.com

All Scripture quotations, unless otherwise indicated, are taken from the Holy Bible, New International Version®, NIV®. Copyright ©1973, 1978, 1984, 2011 by Biblica, Inc.™ Used by permission of Zondervan. All rights reserved worldwide. www.zondervan.com The "NIV" and "New International Version" are trademarks registered in the United States Patent and Trademark Office by Biblica, Inc.™

Scripture quotations marked (NLT) are from Holy Bible, New Living Translation, copyright © 1996, 2004, 2007, 2013, 2015 by Tyndale House Foundation. Used by permission of Tyndale House Publishers Inc., Carol Stream, Illinois 60188. All rights reserved.

Scripture quotations marked (ESV) are from The ESV® Bible (The Holy Bible, English Standard Version®), copyright © 2001 by Crossway, a publishing ministry of Good News Publishers. Used by permission. All rights reserved.

Scripture taken from The Message. Copyright © 1993, 1994, 1995, 1996, 2000, 2001, 2002. Used by permission of NavPress Publishing Group.

Scripture taken from the NEW AMERICAN STANDARD BIBLE®, Copyright © 1960,1962,1963,1968,1971,1972,1973,1975,1977,1995 by The Lockman Foundation. Used by permission.

Edited by Kristin Vanderlip
Cover design by Nobels Design Co.
Cover photo by skinny alien from Pexels
Interior design by Typewriter Creative Co.

ISBN 978-1-7774231-0-0 (Paperback)
ISBN 978-1-7774231-1-7 (eBook)

For Alfred.
My first companion in grief,
the fierce protector of my teenage years,
and my confidante.
Not all who wander are lost.

CONTENTS

FOREWORD

Most of us have dealt with grief in our lives. Many of us have learned that grief follows its own path, is capable of overwhelming our souls, and weakens our resolve to keep going. Grief changes us. Thelma has written a devotional on grief because she knows all of this is true.

As her and her husband's pastor, I can share that this rich and comforting devotional has been forged by the fires of their individual and collective grief. Thelma has faced intense grief in the past with the loss of close family members; with her husband, they continue to face the grief of infertility and Len's incurable disease that keeps him from gainful employment and often leaves him riddled with pain. Not surprisingly then, Thelma writes from a position of authenticity and honesty as a wounded, grieving saint.

Over the years, and by God's grace, Thelma has been able to apprehend the promises of Scripture with great veracity, clarity, and hope to help her with her grief. More specifically, she has come to see the Psalms not simply as an antidote to her grief but as a partner in her grief. Borne of that reality, this devotional on the Psalms is a treasure chest of hope and comfort with its compass pointed to the only One who truly knows our grief—Jesus Christ.

Thelma has a unique writing gift. She sees things that others do not, expresses things that others are not able to put to words. As you read through this devotional, realize it is not to be skimmed and read quickly. Rather, it needs to be read slowly. It needs to be savored and pondered. You need to allow what is shared to find its way into your soul as she mines the deep promises of hope from the book of Psalms.

Wherever you are in your own story of personal grief, this devotional has a word for you. I commend this devotional to you with the prayer that your eyes will be open to the quiet assurances that fill each page!

Ian Wildeboer
Pastor – Mercy Christian Church

INTRODUCTION

"I have been accustomed to call this book, I think not inappropriately, 'An Anatomy of all the Parts of the Soul;' for there is not an emotion of which any one can be conscious that is not here represented as in a mirror. Or rather, the Holy Spirit has here drawn to the life all the griefs, sorrows, fears, doubts, hopes, cares, perplexities, in short, all the distracting emotions with which the minds of men are wont to be agitated."

–John Calvin

O ur walk with God is a whole-body experience. There are those who prefer to hold the context of their faith exclusively in the mind and those who prefer to experience their faith through the varied facets of their emotions. Our tendency to lean toward the extreme of one or the other often leads to disdain or contempt for those who interpret these things differently.

Perhaps a middle course is a truer interpretation found in Scripture. In Mark 12:30, Jesus answers the question about the greatest commandment with these words: "Love the Lord your God with all your heart and with all your soul and with all your mind and with all your strength." Recalling the words of Moses in Deuteronomy 6, Jesus expounds on the whole-hearted, embodied reality of the Christ-follower. God doesn't want just the attention of our minds or the over-flow of our emotions. God wants the entirety of our beings, working in harmony for his service and his glory.

He wants our hearts (*kardia*), the whole of them, with-out simulation or pretense. He demands our souls (*psychē*), the seats of our feelings, desires, affections, and aversions. He wants the engagement of our minds (*dianoia*) to increase our understanding of him, and so increase our desire for him. And he wants us to move our bodies in service toward him with our strength (*ischys*), for the joy of his glory and the support of the Body.

When we attempt to live a half-hearted faith, we ignore the expectations God has on our lives. He created us—in his exquisite omnipotence—to be fully turned toward him in an embodied experience of faith. Where would be our grief over sin and the shattered inadequacy of this world, were it not for our hearts? How would we gain hearts of wisdom without applying our mental faculties to the beauty of God's self-revelation in Scripture? Why would we bend our bodies toward the burdens of others if our abilities were irrelevant?

We can be tempted to turn the inadequate limitations of humanity to deal tenderly with our grief into a direct cor-relation of God's ability to do the same. If we do, however, we limit God's capacity to care about our grief more than any human ever could. Finding ourselves in grief can be a match-less experience. If we are unaccustomed to acknowledging the weight of our emotions and their role in our life, grief can feel like a vast, roiling ocean. We feel forgotten, defeated, exhausted.

The Church has long struggled to normalize the expected facets of grief, and so we still often find ourselves confused by the mental, physical, and spiritual erosion present with grief. We struggle to sleep and force ourselves to eat. Perhaps we eat too much or can't crawl out from under the weighty security of blankets. Perhaps we cannot find the will to weep or cannot stop. Through it all, we are reminded God is good, and our joy is made complete in him, though the darkness of sorrow presses hard on us and the surety of what we believe cracks along the edges.

Grief is the shadow of grace. The grace of Christ Jesus indwells those whose lives are hidden in him and holds the transformative power of life and faith. When we come to truly understand God's grace (Colossians 1:6), we realize grace is not the power to lift us out of our circumstances, but the solid refuge to persevere within them. Grief may linger, and grace upholds. Sorrow threatens to suffocate, and grace is a crisp lung-full of air. Grief stands in the shadow of grace, not as an enemy or blight to be erased, but as the lifelong reminder that we exist in a busted up, disappointing world.

Eradicating grief will not happen on this side of grace. Though we long deeply to feel only joy and never grief, we find in the Psalms ample assurance that our emotions have a safe haven within the comforting arms of our almighty God. We find, as Calvin writes, "an anatomy for all the parts of the soul," an honest acknowledgment of our humanity in the midst of brokenness. We see ourselves in the words written over the course of a thousand years. We hear the echoes of our own cries in the poetry and prayers of men long dead. Human emotion is not counter to faith; it is the means through which we deepen our reliance on God as we grow in the knowledge of who he is and how he loves us.

In the Psalms, we find Immanuel—God with us. Not just in the cleaned-up, tidy prayers of his chosen people but also in the deep cries of sorrow, anger, forgottenness, and pain. We can envision the plight of the psalmist, imagine the pitch and tenor of his plea and questioning, and so hear our own cries. Within the rich beauty of the Psalms, we find this assurance: The God who created us not only knows our grief and suffering, he also wants us to bring those to him— whether that's from the tear-stained pillow in your darkened bedroom, the hot steam of a shower, or crumpled against the kitchen counter, unable to catch your breath in the midst of exhausting sorrow. He wants to hear from us, and he's not worried about the mess.

While this short volume could never do justice to the immense beauty of the collected Psalms, I pray the words rendered here will allow you to discover some language to orient yourself in the midst of tumultuous grief and, in do-ing so, turn you more confidently to seek the face of the One who loves you best.

BLESSED IS...

Psalm 1

The book of Psalms opens with a preface which, when rightly understood, opens our eyes to the true context of the Psalms. Whoever assembled the Psalms into a single volume chose a powerful message to stand at its opening: God's eye is fixed on you, his chosen one.

I spent much of my life misreading Psalm 1. Overwhelm overtakes me as my sins and inadequacies bubble to the surface. Can I consider myself blameless? Do I always choose good company? Do I truly delight in the word of God and meditate upon it day and night? No, I do not.

We miss the point, however, if we mistake this psalm as chastisement rather than encouragement. These brief verses highlight the differences between the godly, the wicked, and the ultimate end of each. It is not meant as a chastisement to do more, do better. Our standing before God is never dependent on our actions or productivity. Often, we want to secure God's favour through a hallmark list of good deeds or be seen as busy and exhausted to highlight how much we care.

God's people ("the blessed ones") are described as trees

"planted," not as wild trees grown from random saplings one spring, but trees chosen with care and rooted in a place of flourishing, near streams of water. We are not the wild underbrush of an overgrown forest, easy to miss, or withering without adequate access to water or sunlight. We are, instead, planted where our roots will sink down into fertile soil, fed by the Living Water himself.

Take particular note of verse 6: "For the Lord watches over the way of the righteous." As Charles Spurgeon writes, "[God] is constantly looking on their way, and though it be often in mist and darkness, yet the Lord knoweth it."[1] The onus here is not on the godly man or woman but rather on the God who guards his or her life. His gaze is fixed on us with omnipotent love. Our well-being and the life we live are of primary concern to him.

The preface to this entire book rests on this: The Lord is attentive to the details of your life. He is incapable and unwilling to look away, whether you are struggling beneath dark waves of grief or shouting praise from the mountains, heart overflowing with joy. The presence of God is the constant in the lives of his people, despite pleasant or dire circumstances. The unchanging, holy nature of his character is the steadfast rock beneath your feet.

And so, the book of Psalms opens with the foundation of Immanuel: our Creator who knows us better than we know ourselves, upholding us in all things. Whether in the mist and darkness or the bright sunshine of beauty, his eye is fixed upon us. We are his beloved, chosen people. This psalm is not meant as a recalcitrant rebuke to live blamelessly, perform at a higher capacity, or strive to earn what we cannot. We are, instead, reminded of who we in the presence of almighty God: righteous and clothed in the white robes of Christ Jesus.

Our worth and value in the eyes of God are set firmly in place before we venture through this prayer psalter. Our circumstances may fluctuate, shaking the ground beneath our feet, but we stand on this assurance and boldly pray the words of Psalm 17:6: "Keep me as the apple of your eye; hide me in the shadow of your wings."

As you walk the tangled road of grief, you may feel as though God is far off; you may imagine yourself forgotten and neglected. May this psalm serve as comfort as you wander through grief. You are never out of God's sight. His eyes are fixed on you, his chosen and beloved child. The violent turbulence of the storm by no means impacts the constancy of his presence. He is well aware of the details of your pain and suffering, and he will hide you in the shadow of his wings (Psalm 91:4).

HE TAKES
IT IN HAND

Psalm 10

When my mother died, I was fifteen years old. My brother and I came home on a cool January evening to find her asleep on the couch. The TV blared in the background as we silently and reluctantly moved toward the realization that she was not, in fact, sleeping. It is no understatement to say my life was ripped apart that night, traumatized by finding her. Grief was a deep, riotous ocean, and I was but a speck of flotsam.

When we are beset by grief, suffering, and pain, our first guttural cry is to God.

"Where are you?"

"How did this happen?"

"Do you even care?"

"How can you be good and yet allow this?"

We hide these questions. We scream them into pillows or wash them down the shower drain in hot, soapy blobs.

We worry our faith will seem shattered and negated by the doubts and questions that arise. It matters, after all, to keep it together, to prove we're not losing it. Settled down, we soothe ourselves dismissively with, "It's not so bad."

And if it is? If the pain is overwhelming, and the grief a hot searing wound, where do these questions belong? What safe place can we run to?

We could start in Psalm 10, where the psalmist brings truly difficult questions and lays them before God.

"Why, Lord, do you stand far off?
Why do you hide yourself in times of trouble?"
(Psalm 10:1)

If you are worried that you are the first person in the course of human history to ask God where on earth he's gone, set those worries aside. Not only are you not the first, but you also will not be the last. And, best of all, the God-breathed words of this psalm have recorded this haunting question for our benefit. It is no new phenomenon for the human heart to find itself immersed in sorrow and doubt God still cares. As Paul David Tripp writes, "The Psalms are in the Bible to keep us honest about the brokenness of our world and the messiness of our faith."[2]

The psalmist draws some beautiful parallels in this psalm. The assault of the wicked on the helpless is drawn in sharp contrast to God's tenderness toward the suffering.

"But you, God, see the trouble of the afflicted;
you consider their grief and take it in hand."
(Psalm 10:14)

He considers your grief. Even when it feels like God is absent and you have been forgotten, God considers your grief and takes it in hand. The original Hebrew for the word "consider" means to "regard with favour or care." Those words spark an image of the soft, loving look of a heavenly Father who adores you and sees your pain. Not only is his tender gaze fixed on you, he is also gently holding your grief in his hands: hands of power and strength; hands capable of carrying and sustaining you.

Your grief is not insignificant to your Creator. He leans into your grief and cradles it with gentle tenderness because he loves you. You are not forgotten. You are not left behind. You are here, holding the gaze of the almighty God who loves to call you his own. He is not afraid of your questions, your fears, or your doubts. He wants to hear from you, to have you bring all of the messiness of faith to the foot of the cross. Yell if you must. Demand to know where he is. Weep, pound the ground, throw things—the violent pain of it all is not a deterrent to his care of you.

> "You, LORD, hear the desire of the afflicted;
> You encourage them, and you listen to their cry." (v.17)

Hear, O Lord, and answer. To be heard is such a simple term in the English language, but, in the Hebrew, it infers both: to be heard and to receive an answer. The answer we are given appears in the next line: encouragement. Reassurance. As we draw near to the God of all comfort, he draws near to us (James 4:8), and, in the presence of God, we receive what we need.

Draw near today in whatever mess you find yourself in, and let the Spirit of comfort soothe and encourage you.

HONEST LAMENT

Psalm 13

Psalm 13 is considered a song of lament. Merriam Webster defines lament as "mourning aloud." Lament is a passionate expression of grief or sorrow. Our Western, North American culture is not particularly familiar with audible mourning, though there are cultures around the world where grief is expressed with both passion and volume.

We North Americans tend to keep grief neat and tidy when out in public. Yes, perhaps we will sob into a pillow late at night or hide in the car at work and weep, but we have been subtly taught to grieve quietly, preferably in private. We are taught it is best to leave our grief at home.

The book of Psalms was God's psalter for his people, and approximately a third of these psalms were written in what we might call a minor key. Songs of lament were meant to be audibly and passionately expressed by his people. They are words of pain, doubt, fear, anger, and loneliness. Our culture may not know what to do with grief, but God does.

Bring it to me, he says. And so, he gives us words meant

for the corporate worship of his chosen people, and we are meant to raise them aloud to him.

"How long, O Lord? How long? How long? How long?"

Author of the book *This Too Shall Last*, K.J. Ramsey, wrote these words:

"Lament names what is broken.
Truth names what is still good.
Faith says both can be true at the same time."

The succinct power of those words is encouraging. As we examine Psalm 13, we see an honest naming of the broken. The psalmist is in a period of pain, carrying sorrow in his heart, feeling misunderstood and forgotten by God. It is evident this has been going on for some time, and the situation is not improving.

At the same time, he is still calling out. He is laying the pain and uncertainty before God and asking the hard questions. You can hear the underlying confidence of God's abiding goodness, despite the long, seemingly unending period of waiting.

In verse 3, the psalmist cries, "Give light to my eyes." I love the thoughts from Spurgeon on this portion of the verse: "that is, let the eye of my faith be clear, that I may see my God in the dark."[3] As we cry out from the dark, we long to be reminded that there is no darkness in God. Indeed, the darkness is not dark to him (Psalm 139:12); the dark is only dark for us.

In this psalm, God weaves together pain and confidence with fatherly comfort. There is beauty in how he draws these deep, guttural questions from a place of raw pain and still holds the psalmist as faithful and trusting.

Speaking your honest lament does not negate your faith. Naming the things in your life that have disappointed, caused pain, created grief—this naming is part of the worship of God's people. If it weren't, one-third of the scriptural psalter would not be written in a minor key. We are allowed to mourn aloud. We are invited to stand in our living rooms, Bible open, and let these honest words pour from our lips. Speak the words:

"This hurts, Lord."

"How long, Lord?"

"I can't do this."

"Where are you?"

Asking hard questions does not mean your faith has vanished. Asking the hard questions means you know where to take them—confident in the one who holds your grief, your hard questions, and the surety of your faith.

With our eyes fixed on Jesus—the author and finisher of our faith—we are allowed to hold his gaze and ask the hard questions. He is not afraid of us naming the painful, broken things in our lives. In fact, he wants to hear you name them, to draw near to him in the sorrow, and allow his comfort to soak into your very being. He may not make everything better overnight, but his mercy will be new each morning.

ANCIENT LAMENT

Psalm 77

Lament, in the Ancient Near East, was often a corporate acknowledgment of grief. As we have already considered, corporate lament is something the Western church has long forgotten, believing grief is best kept private and quiet. It is a strange Western phenomenon to be without an avenue for corporate lament. While physical loss is limited to the graveside and perhaps an hour of corporate gathering, we offer very few (if any) other opportunities for grief to be a communal expression of sorrow.

Whether a fallout from a stoic avoidance of sentimentality or emotional expression, Western Christians often find themselves isolated in their grief. Especially for those who experience ongoing, ambiguous loss, grief is a silent weight they carry alone. We hold ourselves to euphemisms and pick-me-ups:

"Now now, settle down. It's not all bad."

"Go, wash your face. Chin up."

"Others have it far worse than you."

When we find ourselves in a psalm of lament, we need

to remember the Israelites held to a different approach to grief—one we would do well to explore corporately in our modern, dust-yourself-off Christianity. The Archeology Bible provides this insight into Ancient Near East lament: "The custom of languishing in dust and ashes pointed to the fragility of human life and to the inexorable end of all life—a return to dust. Acts that otherwise would have been considered undignified, such as shaving one's head and tearing out one's beard became appropriate expressions of grief."[4]

While our modern culture may not know how to address appropriate expressions of grief, the Psalms show us that the Lord created avenues for his people to grieve. Psalm 77 opens with words of deep pain and anguish. You can almost sense the restless ache within the psalmist, bodily shifting about in discomfort, reaching to the heavens for some response from God. The first four verses of the psalm remind us of all the physical manifestations we experience in grief: weeping, insomnia, exhaustion, and being unable to speak or focus. Grief is not a new phenomenon. Though we may be continually learning new language around our grief, Scripture makes it evident that grief has looked the same across the centuries. We are listless and weary and overwhelmed.

"Has his unfailing love vanished forever? Has his promise failed for a time? Has God forgotten to be merciful?" (vv. 8-9). You can almost hear the disbelief and dismay in the psalmist's voice. Floundering in pain, he struggles to understand why God can feel so absent when everything he knows about God says it is impossible.

As if shaking his head to clear the foggy thoughts, he

returns to recalling the wonders of God. *No*, he declares. *God is a covenant keeper, who stands by his promises and cannot stop loving his people.* He deliberately remembers the deliverance from Egypt, and we find ourselves in verse 19: "Your path led through the sea, your way through the mighty waters, though your footprints were not seen." Recalling the parting of the Red Sea, the psalmist makes a declaration about the abiding presence of God and how it is something we can always count on.

You were there, Lord, even though we couldn't see your footprints. We saw your deliverance at work, though we could not see you. You were the pillar of fire by night and the cooling shade in the heat of the day. You were the manna and the quail, our daily bread. You were the gushing waters at Meribah, our Living Water. You are the man at the well who saw the Samaritan woman and offered her Living Water, your very self. You are the healer of the sick, the deliverance of our souls and our righteousness before God. You are the voice of reassurance to the disciples as you prepared them for your death, and you are our promise of joy. The fingerprints of your intimate care are found in all the details of our lives, even when our weak and weary bodies cannot see them.

Beloved, though his path leads you through the mighty waters and his footprints are not seen, he is here, right beside you. Despite your state of trouble and deep pain, his love has not vanished, nor his promise failed. His mercy for you cannot fail.

DESPERATION

Psalm 88

Many of the psalms close on a note of confident hope. Most of them do, in fact. There are two psalms, however, that end with dark hopelessness: Psalm 39 and Psalm 88. These are the psalms no one wants to talk about. In all the years of sitting in the church pew on Sunday, I don't believe I have ever heard a message on Psalm 39 and only one on Psalm 88.

Why would God even put these two psalms in the most beautiful book of the Bible? Derek Kidner captures it best, I believe: "The very presence of these prayers in Scripture is a witness to God's understanding. God knows how men speak when they are desperate."[5]

If we wanted proof God has no need for us to whitewash our pain, we find it in Psalm 88. We must look no further. If this psalm is an affront to your senses, if its bleak language and abrupt ending make you uncomfortable, be assured God is neither affronted or uncomfortable. More than a commentary on our pain, however, this psalm presents a clear image of who God is.

The psalmist here is a man named Heman (not to be confused with Haman, the villain in the story of Esther), the grandson of Samuel. He was a son of Korah, a Levitical songwriter and musician, and it's widely accepted that the psalms in the 40s were either written by him or under his supervision. He worked closely with David and was considered very wise. Solomon, the wisest of all, was compared to Heman: "He was wiser than anyone else, including Ethan the Ezrahite—wiser than Heman" (1 Kings 4:31).

Perhaps it seems increasingly odd that a man of Heman's standing and wisdom would create a psalm like this, full of despair and despondency. Or perhaps, it was a special dispensation of the Lord to have a man of Heman's standing to declare these words in the midst of his people. As Spurgeon writes, "Holy sorrow ought to be expressed with quite as much care as the most joyful praise… it is more difficult to express sorrow fitly than it is to pour forth notes of gladness."[6]

Based on the psalm, Heman is physically afflicted in some way, perhaps even facing death, which has led to emotional and spiritual affliction. The psalmist lays grievance after grievance before God, demanding an answer or reckoning.

> You have put me in the lowest pit,
> in the darkest depths.
> Your wrath lies heavily on me;
> you have overwhelmed me with all your waves.
> You have taken from me my closest friends
> and have made me repulsive to them.
> I am confined and cannot escape;

my eyes are dim with grief. (vv. 6-9)

Unlike other psalms, there is no shift within the prayer towards God's faithfulness or presence. The psalmist unloads a barrage of complaints against God, a relentless cross-examination. Rather than utilizing the gift for hindsight, the psalmist goes so far as to accuse God of never being faithful or near. He exaggerates the troubles of his youth and closes the prayer with the idea that "Even darkness is a better friend than you, God" (v. 18, paraphrase mine).

God knows how men speak when they are desperate.

So what, then, do we conclude when we read this prayer and flinch at the bombardment of accusation toward God? We understand this: God identifies with those of us who sometimes pray like this. As he is the God of grace and understanding, he knows how we speak when we are desperate. This psalm exists in Scripture, according to Tim Keller, so that we can hear this message: "I am the God of this man, even though he is not getting it right."[7]

He is your God, even when you don't get it right.

He is your God, not just because you slap a happy face on each morning.

He is your God, even when you want to send a shot across the bow that darkness is a better friend.

He is your God, even when you echo the psalmist in Psalm 39, and ask God just to turn away so you can have a moment's peace.

He is your God because he is a God of grace.

In the darkness, in the deep pain of feeling abandoned and alone, let us remember the one who faced the deepest darkness: the One and Only Son who truly was forsaken by God.

> "From noon until three in the afternoon darkness came over all the land. About three in the afternoon Jesus cried out in a loud voice, "Eli, Eli, lema sabachthani?" (which means "My God, my God, why have you forsaken me?")" (Matthew 27:45-46)

Utter darkness beneath the wrath of God. Completely forsaken to bear that wrath alone. Jesus cried out so that we may know, with intense assurance, that he is our God. We will walk through dark times, and we don't have to whitewash that pain. We won't get it right all the time, because we are bankrupt apart from his mercy and grace.

God knows how we speak when we are desperate. Keep calling out to him, beloved. This prayer exists not to justify our anger but to point to the God of grace. He is your God in the light and in the darkness.

THE HELP OF GOD

Psalm 121

The dark thoughts that creep into our hearts and minds during grief are as real as the brain fog that descends. While we may be uncomfortable talking about suicidal ideation, I'm not sure we can have honest conversations about grief without it. When I was sixteen, I went to bed every night wishing I would not wake in the morning. While I was not prepared to take matters into my own hands, the depth and darkness of my grief after losing my mother pressed painfully into the part of me that wanted to be done with life. Each morning when I woke, anger surged within me. A new morning meant I was forced to slog through another day, despite my repeated requests for relief. I wrapped anger around me like a cloak as I went about my days.

My overall disinterest in life convinced me my faith was broken. How could I possibly still believe in a good God when all I wanted was to die and be with my mother? While I never reached the point of considering how I might accomplish my own death (and I thank God for that), we do the bereaved a disservice if we ignore the hard questions and thoughts that arise in the darkest grief and suffering.

We want to view grief as an emotional or spiritual "problem," forgetting the physical manifestations of grief. The brain fog amid grief and suffering is a very real thing, and by "very real," I mean scientifically studied and verified. It has been shown that "several regions of the brain play a role in emotion... involving emotional regulation, memory, multitasking, organization and learning. When you're grieving, a flood of neurochemicals and hormones dance around in your head."[8] If you find yourself stumbling about in a dense haze, unable to hold a thought, remember an appointment, respond to a text, or sit still long enough to read, it's okay. We face specific symptoms (disturbed sleep, loss of appetite, fatigue, anxiety). When those converge, "it stands to reason that you won't absorb your environment the same way you would when you're content."[9] There is grace here, too, for those struggling to connect the dots in the haze of grief.

When grief dims our vision, the psalmist urges us to look up:

"I lift up my eyes to the mountains—
Where does my help come from?
My help comes from the Lord,
The Maker of heaven and earth." (Psalm 121:1-2)

The beautiful words of this psalm are likely familiar, perhaps even memorized. Once again, we see this imagery of lifting our eyes and fixing our gaze on the Lord. Once again, we see a question and an immediate, confident answer: my help comes from the Lord. The remainder of the psalm walks us through the watchful, intimate care of our God over the details of our lives. Night and day his eyes are on us, his attention fixed on our protection and support.

Sometimes, we tend to romanticize what help from the Lord might look like. We are always open to some grand, miraculous show, though God's help mostly arrives in ordinary moments of dark days. Perhaps we over-spiritualize what that looks like, and, in doing so, forget that the love and care of God is often found in the actions of the Body of Christ. While our fellow believers cannot give us peace or watch over us day and night, their willingness to step into places of pain often make them the tangible hands of God's love and grace. One of the ways our Creator helps us is to send in the casserole-makers, the house-cleaners, the sit-quietly-and-listen tea-drinkers.

Thoughts of not wanting to live anymore can be alarming, for both the bereaved and their loved ones. Perhaps we might say things like, "I don't care what happens to me" or "I don't want to live without him/her." Or perhaps we only think those things and never speak them to another soul. My teenage self never told anyone I had no interest in living anymore. I should have told someone. I should have shared with someone other than God that I no longer wanted to be walking around on this green earth.

Declaring, "She would never do that!" or "He has so much to live for" does little to support those who are in such immense pain and sorrow that they long for release. Any release. Life in deep grief can often feel so foreign and unwanted that the bereaved can feel like they don't belong in their life anymore. This isn't a lack of faith or unchecked emotions. This is a matter of the saturating pain of grief and its effects on the entire body. Therefore, for the helpers, it may be best to assume these thoughts are present.

Our help comes from the Lord. Hear me correctly now: Reading your Bible is not some cure-all pill to make all light and bright and merry again. If you are experiencing suicidal ideation, the Bible is not some magic button to push to make those thoughts disappear. You need to reach out and talk to someone. *Please.*

The Lord's help takes many shapes and forms. Perhaps his support will come through qualified medical care and licensed therapists. Maybe a friend who is a few steps ahead on the road of grief will be able to sit with you in your pain and give you a safe space to talk. Perhaps the Body of Christ will show up to help you rest, eat, and lift your eyes to Jesus. Maybe the Body will show on your doorstep to kneel in prayer with and for you. The Lord's help is rarely an intangible, invisible thing. Most often, it shows up in the flesh and blood of your brothers and sisters in Christ.

Look to the mountains, my friend, and witness the Lord bestow his support and assistance from Zion. Speak your mind in the safety of those who love you and allow them to be the hands and feet of Jesus. Your faith is not broken; you are grieving. Be honest and aware of the whole-body experience of sorrow and allow the gentle arms of Love Everlasting to love you as only he can.

RAGING WATERS

Psalm 69

Perhaps in your grief you have come across well-meaning people who have urged you to replace your grief with the reading of more Scripture or more prayer. As the Western church has set aside corporate lament, we often run into something called "spiritual bypassing" in its place. Spiritual bypassing is a response that suggests our faith can override our grief. It might sound like, "Don't be sad! God is good!" or "Just ask God to take your sadness away!"

Spiritual bypassing has its heart in a misunderstanding about pain, loss, and sorrow. It serves to push us to see ourselves exclusively as spiritual beings and that the responses of the physical body (especially our emotions) are to be avoided or numbed at all costs. Spiritual bypassing holds to the idea that being able to spin every situation to a positive is a faith-filled response to pain. If a reversal of our circumstances is not possible, we must do our best to pretend all is well.

Scripture paints a far different story. While the Christian life is filled with a joy that has no answer here on earth, our walk with Jesus was never intended to be one filled with roses, confetti, and endless laughter. Instead, we were promised "trouble," with the anchoring comfort that Jesus has "overcome the world" (John 16:33). So long as we live and breathe on this side of eternity, our physical and spiritual selves will encounter pain, rejection, scorn, and grief. Creation groans in anticipation of its restoration (Romans 8:22), and we are created beings living in a broken and busted up world.

Psalm 69 is a beautiful example of this world's trouble met with the unafraid love and presence of God. It opens with imagery of drowning, desperation and exhaustion setting in. The opening words of David's prayer are simply this: "Save me, O God." *Save me. Help. I am drowning here, and I can't fight much longer.* While David has provided no specific circumstances to the writing of this psalm, it is evident that the "deep waters" (v. 2) are threatening to be his undoing.

It is apparent that David is the object of scorn and ridicule in this psalm. Within it, we find echoes of Jesus on the cross, our suffering Saviour who endured the mocking, scorn, and ridicule of those who stood nearby. "They put gall in my food," David writes, "and gave me vinegar for my thirst." (v. 21)

David writes about how the usually appropriate expressions of lament (putting on sackcloth, weeping, and fasting) are met with laughter and insults. Nowhere in the psalm is there a sudden reversal of circumstances; by all accounts, David continues to be the object of scorn and shame. Note, however, how he stands in the midst of it and does two things:

1. He acknowledges the depth of the pain. By using the language of drowning, it is evident this is no small situation. "Scorn has broken my heart and left me helpless," he writes in verse 20. "I looked for sympathy and there was none, for comforters but I found none." He is surrounded by circumstances so overwhelming he likens it to drowning: His lungs burning for air, his body fighting to remain at the surface.

2. He asserts his confidence in God by demanding his presence. "Come near and rescue me!" (v. 18); "answer me quickly" (v. 17); "protect me!" (v. 29). The confidence David asserts at the close of the psalm is evident throughout the darker verses as well.

One does not speak desperation into the darkness and suddenly remember God is the one who saves. Rather, David speaks desperation into darkness because he knows God is the only one who saves. He has not forgotten, despite the dumpster fire of his circumstances. From the outset of the psalm, David cries out to the only one who can save him.

Spiritual bypassing might suggest we need to tidy ourselves up and get our theological ducks in a row before we kneel before God. David (and the Holy Spirit, by canonizing these darker psalms) shows us God does not care as much about that as we think he does. Cry out when you're drowning. God already knows the waters are engulfing you and the mouth of the pit is closing above you. There is no point in your life where God is uncertain about whether or not you need deliverance. He would not have sent his only

Son to the cross had our constant need for saving been a question mark. Our need for a Saviour is always pressing, and no amount of whitewashing our pain will minimize it.

Cry out, beloved, from the depth of the pain, from the darkness, from the rising waters. Simply cry out. If the only prayer you can manage for weeks on end is, "Save me, O God!" that's okay. He is already at work.

THE HEART'S CRY

Psalm 25

As I was writing these devotions, I had the opportunity to utilize my pastor's office, a quiet, private space where I could get some work done. I spent the first 20 minutes thoroughly distracted by his walls of books. To my utter delight, I happened upon Spurgeon's *The Treasury of David*—his exhaustive, expository work on the Psalms. In it, Spurgeon writes:

> In these busy days, it would be greatly to the spiritual profit of Christian men if they were more familiar with the Book of Psalms, in which they would find a complete armory for life's battles, and a perfect supply for life's needs. Here we have both delight and usefulness, consolation and instruction. For every condition there is a Psalm, suitable and elevating.[10]

For every condition, there is a psalm. What grace it is that our Abba Father would craft such a remarkable book over a period of 800 years so that even now, centuries later, we would find reflections of our own souls within its pages.

What grace!

In one of the darkest periods of my life, the words of Psalm 25 were the only prayer I could muster. Each morning I would open my Bible and trace the words on the page until my heart had memorized them.

How often do we wish we could say, like David, that our eyes are ever on the Lord? I happen to think they never fully are. As much as we would like to be able to claim that, I think we are often prone to allow our gaze to slip, especially when the storm rolls in and the trouble of this sin-shattered world stains the edges of our hearts.

The imagery of fixing our eyes on the Lord is a beautiful constant throughout the entirety of Scripture. From Jehoshaphat's prayer, "We do not know what to do but our eyes are on you." (2 Chronicles 20:12) to the exhortation to fix our eyes on Jesus (Hebrews 12:2). This repetitive narrative within Scripture is about not only where our gaze should be but also a faithful reassurance that God's eyes are always on us. Despite our concern that he has turned away or failed to see our circumstances, we are reminded time and time again that he is not easily distracted.

In a period when I had no other words to pray, these verses played on repeat within my heart:

> Turn to me and have mercy,
> for I am alone and in deep distress.
> My problems go from bad to worse.
> Oh, save me from them all!
> Feel my pain and see my trouble.
> Forgive all my sins. (Psalm 25:16-18 NLT)

Turn to me. Can you see me? Do you see this pain I'm in? It's not getting any better. See my trouble, Lord. Please. Tell me you see it, and I haven't slipped from your attention.

The cry of the troubled heart is condensed into these three verses in Psalm 25. David lays out what we most desire: to be seen, to be assured of God's presence and attention, and to know that in him, we have grace and mercy in our time of need.

Wherever grief has brought you, you are seen, held, and loved. If, for a time, the only prayer you can muster are these words from Psalm 25, they have been crafted for just that purpose. When it feels like grief has darkened your whole world, remember we call upon a Saviour who suffered, who walked this world in our flesh, and knows the pain of being human. He hears your cries with perfect love and sympathy, and he is near you in all things.

HE BINDS OUR BROKEN HEARTS

Psalm 147

can't tell you how many times I've sat across from women sharing their stories, opening up about their pain to someone who understands. I am so grateful they trust me to hold space for their pain, and, in these conversations, I listen for threads of commonality.

"Am I ever going to be myself again?"

This is the most common question I hear in conversations about grief, and the pain is almost palpable. When my husband and I happily set out to add children to our family, we were brightly expectant and eager. We had watched other families bloom and grow and witnessed successful pregnancies and red-faced babies fresh from the oven. We knew how this worked. We were excited.

Infertility feels much like a steel door being slammed on our fingers. We are shocked when this thing that is supposed to be the most natural thing in the world turns out to be so difficult. We stumble backward to try and reorient, trying to make sense of what is happening. And then, most often, we plunge forward. *We will fix this! This will not be our story!*

And yet, in the fixing, we find ourselves irrevocably broken. We are all likely familiar with the verse, "The Lord is close to the broken-hearted," from Psalm 34, but my heart is drawn more frequently to verse 3 of Psalm 147: "He heals the broken-hearted and binds up their wounds." Scripture does not downplay the devastation that this fallen world can wreak on our fragile spirits. God is not impassive in our sorrow, our brokenness.

Broken-hearted. The original Hebrew word depicts devastation. Its imagery is a violent rending, crushing, and shattering. The same root Hebrew word is used to describe Moses smashing the tablets of the law when he was confronted by Israel's idolatry with the golden calf. Hollywood has twisted a broken heart into something trite and melodramatic, but Scripture outright rejects such shallow depictions. The broken-hearted are changed by their sorrow. They are the jagged remnants of their whole selves.

The verbs in these passages belong to the Lord—he is near, he saves, he heals, and he binds up. The original Hebrew sketches beautiful details into these broad brushstrokes. These are images of the Lord drawing near to the sorrowful heart, gathering the crushed and shattered pieces, and literally piecing his beloved back together. He mends by stitching. He applies compress and bandage. He who made us heals as only he can.

When our hearts are broken, Scripture does not mince words about the severity and pain. We are changed by our sorrow, and while we may not move ON from grief, the Lord binds us with his healing touch so we can move forward WITH our grief. His tenderness toward you is clearly etched onto the pages of Scripture.

Will you ever be the same again? Probably not. Perhaps that's not the answer you wanted to hear. Just as when we glue together a piece of broken pottery, it never looks quite the same. The cracks show, and we may need to handle ourselves with extra care. We are stitched back together, and grief becomes a new thing we carry with us; healing, most often, is not a reversal to a former state but a gradual easing into a new way of being, coping, and feeling.

But here is the promise of your Abba Father:

"the Lord delights in those who fear him,
who put their hope in his unfailing love." (v. 11)

He delights in you, beloved. The power to heal is his, and while you may emerge from this thing called grief a person you are not familiar with, the Lord is drawing near and piecing you back together.

GRIEF IS NOT SIN

Psalm 32

Grief is not sin.

Let me say that again: grief is not sin. We have a tendency to divide the darker emotions (anger, grief, depression) and the sweeter emotions (happiness, joy, elation) on a faith scale, prioritizing the positive emotions as stronger evidence of a thriving faith. Despite the range of emotions we were created with, grief, in and of itself, is not sin.

What evidence do we have, you might ask? Well, the life and ministry of Jesus is the strongest case to illustrate this truth. Our sinless Saviour, who lived the life of perfect obedience to the Father, experienced the depth of human emotion while inhabiting this earthly tent. He was moved to compassion (Matthew 9:36). He was angry (John 2:17). He grieved (John 11).

At the tomb of Lazarus, Jesus wept. The Son of God cried real tears of sorrow because his friend had died, the same way we weep in our own grief. Had this expression of pain and loss been a sin, our Saviour's work on the cross would be irrelevant, for he had failed to live a life of obedience to the Father. Grief is not a sin because Jesus wept.

In Psalm 32, we are met with language that mirrors the bodily weight of grief but used in relation to unconfessed sin. Perhaps from this, we would like to conclude that the two are necessarily related, synonymous even. David writes of "his bones wasting away" (v. 3) and how his "strength was sapped as in the heat of summer" (v. 4). These are words used elsewhere in the Psalms to describe suffering, loss, and trouble.

Here, however, David draws a direct correlation to his bodily condition and unconfessed sin: "Then I acknowledged my sin to you, and did not cover up my inquiry. I said, 'I will confess my transgressions to the Lord.' And you forgave the guilt of my sin" (Psalm 32:5). Sin is apparent in all that we do, think, and say. Our ever-pressing need for a Saviour who forgives weighs heavily upon us, and we find solace and relief when we draw near to God and lay the details of our sin before him.

We are often more willing to point out the sin in others' lives than we are to humbly confess our own sins. "He is stuck in grief," we say. "He needs to move on." Our critical awareness of the pain of others is often accompanied by a solution we fail to grasp ourselves.

While grief itself is not sin, it is possible to sin within grief. On the flip side, it is equally easy to sin within the sweeter emotions. Perhaps in our joy, we flaunt our possessions from a place of pride and superiority. Perhaps we mock those who have less, celebrating our blessings in the context of our work ethic and scorning those we deem lazy. Perhaps, in grief, we lash out repeatedly in anger and bitterness. Perhaps we push everyone away in our pain, longing to sit alone in the darkness and avoid all communion with the Body of Christ.

Sin creeps into every emotion. Psalm 4:4 chides, "In your anger, do not sin." In truth, we could insert any emotion there. In your *joy*, do not sin. In your *sorrow*, do not sin. In your *celebration*, do not sin. The emotion in question is not the point; the resulting action is. How we choose to deal with the broad range of emotions comes down to one thing: do not sin, or, as modeled in Psalm 32, be quick to confess.

Repentance, in Scripture, is the act of turning away from sin and toward the face of God. As we read again and again in the Psalms, God's eyes never turn away from us. When we turn to seek his face, we are not met with his back. We do not need to plead with him to around and look at us. In response to confession, Psalm 32 continues with the promises of God: "I will instruct you and teach you in the way you should go; I will counsel you with my loving eye on you." (v. 8) His gaze remains fixed on us. He remains at the ready with his counsel and love.

In Christ Jesus, we have a sympathetic Saviour. Not only did he experience the wide range of emotions we experience in these dusty human bodies, he also did what we could not do: lived a perfectly obedient life to secure life everlasting. As the writer of Hebrews urges us, we can boldly approach the throne of grace, "so that we may receive mercy and find grace to help us in our time of need" (4:16). With confidence, we can say grief is not sin. Though, within our grief, we may stumble, with confidence we can lean heavily on the shed blood and broken body of our Saviour. He knows our weakness, after all. We are human, after all, and wrought with frailty. Blessed is he who, with the psalmist, can declare, "You are my hiding place; you will protect me from trouble and surround me with songs of deliverance." (v. 7)

MERCY WINS

Psalm 40

"Mercy," A.W. Tozer writes, "is not something God has but something God is."

We find ourselves in a psalm soaked with the mercy of God. From the opening chords, the psalmist lauds the saving mercy of God Most High—lifting from the pit, out of the slime and the muck, providing a firm place to stand, and placing a new song in his heart. David sings of a complete reversal of his spiritual situation in concrete terms we can visualize and relate to.

Our lives often make more sense when we look back on them through the lens of hindsight. We look back, and, as our tears dry, we can trace the footsteps of God in the sand behind us. While we could not always see clearly amid deep sorrow, hindsight is a quiet gift of perspective we can be thankful for.

In this psalm, David moves from personal thanksgiving to a commentary of God's goodness. He then speaks of dedicating his life to the will of God and closes with a prayer for deliverance from suffering and trouble: "Do not withhold your mercy from me, Lord; may your love and faithfulness always protect me." (v. 11)

For God to withhold mercy is for God to withhold his very self. He is unable to be anything other than merciful, for his holy character demands his mercy be readily available to those who seek protection under his wings. When David prays and asks God not to withhold his mercy, he is not speaking from a place where God might actually do that. Rather, he stands on the firm foundation of God's revelation about who he is and asks God to remember. This plea stems from a faith that believes God is who he says he is. *"You have revealed your mercy to me, Lord, time and time again. Please, soak me in your mercy now in my time of trouble."* We can take heart from David's boldness. Even when surrounded by trouble and despair (*My heart fails within me!*), we can be assured of the protection and mercy of our God.

There are times when we speak more of grace than mercy; perhaps, in some ways, we see this as a new covenant shift because of what we already possess in Christ Jesus. In a purely definitive sense, mercy is the withholding of deserved punishment. When sin is held up against the justice of Holy God, the cost of that sin ought to be death (Romans 6:23), yet God withholds the deserved wages of sin. This is mercy.

Grace is a more significant concept in that it encompasses not only the withholding of deserved penalty but also lavishing the guilty with something not deserved. Grace is the freely given, transformative power poured into our lives through Jesus; it's designed to grant us everything we could never earn. Grace is costly and abundant—costly in God sacrificing his only begotten Son, and abundant in the riches it pours into our lives.

We daily remain in need of both mercy and grace. In Christ, we can live confidently in the unmerited favour of God, as Christ stands in heaven as righteousness on our behalf (2 Corinthians 5:21). Despite such a remarkable reversal of spiritual status, our need for him is no less desperate. In Lamentations, we find the words of Jeremiah: "Because of the Lord's great love we are not consumed, for his compassions never fail. They are new every morning; great is your faithfulness" (3:22-23). His mercies are new every morning! And they are new every morning because, each and every day, we use up every last drop of the Lord's mercy, and we desperately need a refill each morning when our feet hit the floor.

David knew this truth as well, without the benefit of knowing Christ as his Lord and Saviour. As he closes this psalm, he sings, "But as for me, I am poor and needy; may the Lord think of me. You are my help and my deliverer; you are my God, do not delay." (v.17)

As we stumble about in our grief and sorrow, let us ask God to help us to remember this: He is who he says he is, and his mercies are new each morning. By the Lord's great love, we are not consumed, or, as Paul writes to the Corinthians:

> We now have this light shining in our hearts, but we ourselves are like fragile clay jars containing this great treasure. This makes it clear that our great power is from God, not from ourselves. We are pressed on every side by troubles, but we are not crushed. We are

perplexed, but not drive to despair. We are hunted down, but never abandoned by God. We get knocked down, but we are not destroyed. Through suffering, our bodies continue to share in the death of Jesus so that the life of Jesus may also be seen in our bodies. (2 Corinthians 4: 7-9 NLT)

STAND ON THE PROMISES

Psalm 31

There are many psalms where we are invited to stand boldly and hold out God's promises to him, urging him to remember his faithfulness toward us, but the weaving of Psalm 31 does this in such a profound, meaningful way. A beautiful blend of distress and confidence, this psalm has been a source of comfort and prayer during many sorrowful times.

In the deep, murky trenches of infertility, I found myself continually wondering about the *when*. *When* would we have children? *When* would God allow the growth of our family? I would confidently declare the words of verses 14 and 15: "But I trust in you, Lord, I say, 'You are my God.' My times are in your hands." It became a prayer of confidence. *Whenever the babies come, Lord, I'm ready. I can wait. Your timing, not mine.*

In the days when I could barely rise from my knees beneath the crippling weight of grief, I would cry out, "Be merciful to me, Lord, for I am in distress; my eyes grow weak with sorrow."

It is not bravado that allows us to stand and hold God to his promises. Honest faith asks God to be who he has shown himself to be: near, faithful, good. Quiet humility accepts he is all of those things, even when our circumstances do not correct themselves. Taking a firm stand on God's promises does not mean we are testing or challenging God. Rather, it means that we are believing that who God is and has declared himself to be is a far greater constant than our ever-shifting circumstances.

And oh, the rich beauty of those promises. Consider these powerful verses from the Book of Isaiah:

> But now, this is what the Lord says—
> he who created you, Jacob,
> he who formed you, Israel:
> "Do not fear, for I have redeemed you;
> I have summoned you by name; you are mine.
> When you pass through the waters,
> I will be with you;
> and when you pass through the rivers,
> they will not sweep over you.
> When you walk through the fire,
> you will not be burned;
> the flames will not set you ablaze.
> For I am the Lord your God,
> the Holy One of Israel, your Savior;
> I give Egypt for your ransom,
> Cush and Seba in your stead.

Since you are precious and honored in my sight,
and because I love you,
I will give people in exchange for you,
nations in exchange for your life. (Isaiah 43:1-4)

The assurance of these verses is a gift when we walk through fire or pass through the waters. And why? Because we are his, precious and honoured in his sight. As much as God uses Isaiah to reassure the Israelites (and us, today) of his protection, he also makes sure we know to whom we belong. More than that, we have what Israel deeply yearned for: the ultimate Promise wrapped in skin and bone. In Christ, we are the adopted heirs, and he our elder brother. "See what kind of love the Father has given to us, that we should be called children of God; and so we are." (1 John 3:1 ESV.) *And so we are.*

When we stand on the assurance of God's promises, we can build a life on the steadfast rock of his character. We can take God at his word. He is who he has revealed himself to be, and within that truth we may also build our lives on the assurance of who he has made us: beloved children of God. Regardless of how our circumstances may quake beneath our feet, he is our rock and our refuge.

REFUGE

Psalm 31

As a modern, first-world civilization, we don't really have a good sense of what it means for God to be a rock and a refuge. For the most part, we live in cities built without walls or in the wide expanse of the country, rolling hills and patchwork farmland all around. Either way, we live in relative freedom and ease, and the idea of having to flee to a place of refuge is largely foreign to us.

Years ago, I went to a paintball field with a large group of friends. Hiding behind trees, ducking behind rocks and dodging paint pellets was an incredible amount of fun, though not entirely harmless, perhaps, as evidenced by the welts I took home that day. There was one rock on the field that provided perfect cover. Flanked by a cliff of sorts, I crouched behind the large boulder that sheltered me from a spray of paint pellets. I was safe, but I could still see and aim when needed.

For those who sang David's psalms, the idea of fleeing to safety was a more accessible metaphor. If Israel were at war, the people would flee to the protection of city walls.

Marauding soldiers raiding farmlands would send people fleeing to caves and foothills to find places to hide. The imagery of God as a rock and a refuge would have immediately filled them with a sense of security and safety.

When we find ourselves assaulted by trouble, where do we go? We can flee to a variety of safe spaces. Perhaps we tuck ourselves in at home, run into the arms of a loved one, reach for comfort food, or busy ourselves with an activity that soothes us.

David uses two words for safety here: rescue and refuge. Rescue is often considered as a lifting above our troubles. A rescue helicopter hovers over raging waves to save a stranded, waterlogged swimmer. Refuge, on the other hand, conveys an image of being held safely within our current situation. We climb into a cave to escape; we hunker down behind a boulder and wait for danger to pass. David asks for both in the opening verses of Psalm 31—he desires to be rescued and sheltered, for he knows that God can do both. God could alter his circumstances and remove them from him, or God could wrap him safely in the midst of trouble, saving him in a whole different way.

While we long for the opportunity to live our best life now, we can find ourselves treading paths of pain and suffering we did not choose. We want nothing more than an end to the storm. Seasons of life, we call them—these periods of darkness that press in and smother. Using the words "seasons" is so telling of our mindset when it comes to walking with trouble: *It will end. This pain will not last forever. This, too, shall pass. Very soon, I will be able to look back, and it will be over.*

Except... when it's not. When pain lingers. When the baby doesn't come. When an illness has no cure. When an accident causes permanent physical damage. When the ultrasound tech cannot find the heartbeat. When the debilitation of mental illness scuffs the edges of every day. When relationships remain strained or estranged.

What we blithely refer to as a season can become a new normal with no evident rescue on the horizon. Our deep desire for rescue can lead us to forget refuge. In Psalm 31, David prays, as Matthew Henry puts it, "that if [God] did not immediately deliver him out of his troubles, yet he would protect and shelter him in his troubles"[11]

These verses of Psalm 31 remind me also of Zephaniah 3:17:

> The Lord your God is in your midst,
> a mighty one who will save;
> he will rejoice over you with gladness;
> he will quiet you by his love;
> he will exult over you with loud singing.

He will quiet you by his love. Imagine a small child in the powerful embrace of a loving, gentle Father. Imagine him rocking the child the way a mother might rock a toddler, singing softly and with great tenderness, quieting him or her with patience and comfort.

Let us remember to pray confidently for both refuge and rescue. David asked God for both, and we can too. And, in response to that prayer, God, like a mighty warrior and our Abba Father, will cradle and quiet you with his love.

THE
TRUSTWORTHY ONE

Psalm 31

How would you characterize your trust in God? I don't know about you, but I am not particularly good at trusting. My high school drama teacher (who also just happened to be my father) would regularly have the class practice trust falls with each other. This is not a game that I play well, and, if memory serves me correctly, I managed never to complete a trust fall in my high school drama career. *Catch people? Sure thing! I'm there! Have people catch me? No, thank you very much.*

It's probably no wonder that my relationship of trust with God has been a rocky mess. In a desperate session with my counselor, I blurted out my deepest confession, "He hasn't dropped me yet, but that doesn't mean he isn't going to." Somehow, my trust in God had been reduced to this horrible high school drama exercise, and I was waiting, breath bated, for God to miss his cue.

And yet, some of my favourite verses of Psalm 31 are

verses 14-16:

> But I trust in you, Lord;
> I say, "You are my God."
> My times are in your hands;
> deliver me from the hands of my enemies,
> from those who pursue me.
> Let your face shine on your servant;
> save me in your unfailing love.

Perhaps you, like me, struggle with trust. Perhaps this walk down the road of grief has been so bumpy that your trust is looking a little bedraggled and dented. Perhaps you are trying to fake it 'til you make it and hope that everything is relatively intact when you come out of this.

Can I share a little secret?

Trusting God has less to do with WHAT we hope he does (drop us or catch us) and much more to do with WHO we believe God is. As I explored my trust issues, I realized I didn't believe God was trustworthy. I doubted his faithfulness. The witness of my own life was not adequate to cement my faith and rest in the assurance that he would not drop me. Even when life was going well, I waited nervously for the other shoe to drop, as it were, because I believed God was capricious and unpredictable. I allowed my experience to dictate the image of the God I thought I believed in, and everything was collapsing around me.

Trusting God also had a lot to do with how I imagined he viewed me. I was a slow learner, and so I needed to sit beneath the weight of trial after trial until I learned some specific lesson. Since I seemed to be experiencing ongoing suffering, I assumed I was too stupid to figure out what on earth he was trying to teach me. Again, I allowed my experience to inform my belief rather than relying on Scripture. I do that a lot, and it's always gotten me in trouble. When we walk through dark days, it is not because we've been too slow to catch on to some elusive lesson God is trying to teach us. He is not some cruel taskmaster holding our feet to the fire until we finally catch on.

Often, we forget in the dark what we know to be truth in the light. In our weakness, we envision God as a stern father, quick to punish, and look to Jesus as the tender, smiling Shepherd. We forget, then, that Jesus is the perfect representation of the Father in every way, and that anyone who has seen Jesus, has seen the Father (John 14:9). What we see in the life and ministry of Jesus is true of the Father. And what we see in the Father is true of the Son.

Eventually, I boiled it down to two summary statements:

God is who he says he is.

God loves me because he says he does.

If I could decide to take God at his word, I could be confident that he wouldn't drop me. This shift in thinking has been revolutionary for my faith life, and it was not long afterward that I had the word "beloved" tattooed on my inner wrist.

I am beloved of God, and that means everything, because he says so.

You are beloved of God, and that means everything because he says so.

ONLY ONE GIFT

Psalm 31

So often, when we walk through dark, difficult times, we can find ourselves looking for a single answer. A single, good gift. A reprieve. A lessening of grief. An escape. A hiding place. In infertility, we find ourselves fixated on one thing: a baby. In singleness, we desire a spouse. Perhaps in grief, we simply long for a day when we do not wake in pain. With chronic pain or illness, we hunger for a cure or a medicine to manage symptoms effectively.

In verse 19 of Psalm 31, David declares:

How abundant are the good things
that you have stored up for those who fear you,
that you bestow in the sight of all,
on those who take refuge in you.

While I'm not a regular user of The Message translation of the Bible, I love how Eugene Peterson paraphrases this verse:

What a stack of blessing you have piled up

for those who worship you,

Ready and waiting for all who run to you.

A stack of blessings. An abundance of good things.

There was a time when I responded to this verse with a sulky mutter: "That's great, Lord. I just want a baby. You can keep all the other stuff." I wanted only one gift—and that gift was being withheld. A part of me thought I was actually a martyr, denying myself all good things while hoping for motherhood. *Just give me this one thing, Lord, and I'll never ask you for anything again.*

Perhaps you've caught yourself in this train of thinking. Perhaps you've found yourself bargaining with God as if he were a vendor at a flea market: *I'll take these two, but you have to throw this in for free.* Or, *I just want THIS one... you can keep the other two.* We can have some pretty fixed ideas about what the good things in our lives should look like. In many ways, our gauge for evaluating these good gifts exists in comparison with others.

She has three children... why can't I have just one?

Their house is beautiful... why can't I have a big, new home like theirs?

She has kids AND a career... I have a job I hate and no kids. How is this fair?

He's had the same steady job for over a decade... I can barely put food on the table.

We can find ourselves operating within a transactional gospel, almost without noticing. This idea of praising God when times are sweet and enjoyable while also believing the absence of good things indicates God's disfavour is a strong marker of living with a transactional faith.

Consider the opening act of the book of Job where we find Satan suggesting Job's righteousness was purely transactional: "He only loves you because he has all this beautiful stuff, God. Take that way, and he'll curse your name" (Job 1:10, paraphrase mine). While we cannot fully fathom why God allows Satan to wreak utter chaos on Job, he does.

And so, Job sits outside the city, grieving the death of his children, the devastation of his life, and the abandonment of his wife. Covered in a contagious, infectious disease, he also has to sit through countless rejoinders of bad theology by his friends. Had Satan been right, and his righteousness before God was dependent on lavish blessing, Job might not have hesitated in throwing in the towel and cursing God.

Don't we feel the same, sometimes? We find ourselves in desperate times and wonder what we did wrong? Or we recount all the ways we've done things correctly and try to understand why we aren't floating in delicious blessing and joy. We carry within us the desire to believe suffering is directly related to our behaviour, because if it is, we can work our way out of it. We can work our way back to God's good graces and set things right in our world again.

The good he has in store for us may look nothing like we expected. The blessing with your name on it may not look like you were hoping. When we design our expected blessings to look like our neighbour's blessings, we run the risk of missing out on what God is already giving us. When we hold so tightly to our desire for one good gift, we fail to have hands open to receive all the rest. When we desire one thing so deeply, our eyes tend to slip closed to every other gift our Abba Father is pouring into our lives.

The way that friend tried to step into your pain and be present.

The kind words from your boss on a job well done.

The way your spouse leaned in for a kiss at the movies.

The gift card a brother in Christ slipped you at church.

God desires to give good gifts to all his children, my friend. Even to you. He has a storehouse full of them—blessings stacked high, one upon another. Not one of those blessings is dependent on your ability to get everything right or stay out of trouble. Neither are those blessings withheld in the midst of pain or suffering. Our circumstances have no bearing on the Lord's lavish generosity. He will faithfully pour his love and blessing into your life, even when those blessings look far different than you were hoping.

HE IS MINE

Psalm 27

As I researched and studied the psalms, I was surprised by how many commentators and preachers made some variation on this statement: the Psalms are here to keep us honest. In the Psalms we are confronted by trouble and sorrow, jubilant joy and astonishing hope. We hear the hard questions and find solid footing in age-hold assurance. As Paul David Tripp states, "The psalms are unsettling and messy and honest."

When we find ourselves in the midst of grief or suffering, we end up preaching ourselves one kind of gospel or another. While outwardly we may say all the correct phrases to ease the hearts and minds of those around us, inwardly we may be singing another tune. If we have convinced ourselves that God is other than who he says he is, our perseverance within grief and suffering will falter.

Psalm 27 is one of those beautiful psalms that weaves the cries of a troubled heart with golden threads of sweet theology. Biblical faith, we learn in this psalm, never ever asks you to deny reality or gloss over the trouble in your life. We don't protect God's reputation by faking it until we make it. We are invited to stand in honest community, believing that the glorious grandeur of God surpasses any darkness we find ourselves in.

As the psalm opens, we find a declaration of confidence:

The Lord is my light and my salvation—whom shall I fear?
The Lord is the stronghold of my life—of whom shall I be afraid? (v.1)

Take careful note of the repetition of the word "my." This is no impersonal, abstract declaration. While it is equally true to list these attributes of God in a general sense (he is light, salvation, stronghold), it is sweet delight and comfort to find that we can absorb these truths personally. Scripture is meant to be deeply personal, teaching us not only who God is, but also to teach us who we are as his children. Thanks to intentional, sovereign grace, each child of God can say that God is these things to ME. Through God's glorious grace, I have unrestricted access to God and can claim who he is for myself personally.

The gospel we preach to ourselves is not always the gospel we find in Scripture. Perhaps we revert to a gospel of self-reliance, believing we are meant to push through on our power, and prove we can survive whatever is thrown at us. Perhaps we find ourselves believing God is far off and impersonal, the trials in our life evidence of his disinterest. Or maybe we find ourselves telling ourselves God's grace is limited by our goodness, our ability to get things right, and prove we are worthy of his generosity.

When we find ourselves tucking these false gospels into our hearts as a means of survival, everything begins to crumble. Self-reliance pushes back against community and the support of the Body of Christ. A jumbled view of God sets our feet to wandering, seeking some kind of counterfeit god who feels more personal and near. Pressing hard into a "do good" life sets us on a path of exhaustion and turmoil, as we strive towards constant self-improvement and competition to earn what is already ours. Living for a false gospel will always lead to despair.

> "I will say of the Lord, "He is my refuge and my fortress, my God, in whom I trust."" (Psalm 91:2)

Scripture overflows with these personal declarations of who God is. *He is mine. You are my God, my refuge, my fortress, my light, my salvation, my stronghold.* During his time on earth, Jesus echoed the same gospel: ""I am the good shepherd; I know my sheep and my sheep know me" (John 10:14). The gospel remains the same throughout Scripture: God is ours and we are his. When the dark creeps in and we silently preach false gospels to ourselves, may we cling to these personal pronoun, both the old and the new.

SEEK HIS BEAUTY

Psalm 27

hy, in moments of deep trouble, does David want to flee to the temple and gaze upon the beauty of the Lord? David knows and believes a foundational truth: There exists in the universe an awesome and glorious beauty far more beautiful than any ugly thing you will face in your life. Paul David Tripp writes these words: "Peace in life—specifically peace in times of trouble—is found not in the ease of circumstances, but in sound Biblical theology. It is rooted in the worship of God."

In times of turmoil and darkness, David longs to worship God. He longs to seek the beauty of his face (v. 4), knowing both the presence and worship of God is a balm to the soul like no other.

When you see your troubles through the lens of the stunning beauty of the Lord you see life accurately. Where you look is where you'll land. If your eyes are fixed solely on the pain and sorrow in your life, you will see only darkness. If your eyes are fixed on the majesty and beauty of God, your circumstances may not change, but the perspective of your heart certainly will.

Consider Peter for a moment. After feeding the five thousand on the mountainside, Jesus sends his disciples off across the lake of Galilee and spends some time alone in prayer. During the night, a storm sweeps over the water and the disciples are having a difficult time handling the boat. Jesus steps out onto the lake and walks towards them, and these seasoned fishermen are terrified as he approaches.

Only Matthew's account of Jesus walking on water includes Peter's audacious demand to walk on water as well. When he realizes it is Jesus coming toward him, he cries, "Lord, if it's you... tell me to come to you on the water" (Matthew 14:28). Jesus invites him to come to him, and Peter steps out of the boat into the stormy water:

> Then Peter got down out of the boat, walked on the water and came toward Jesus. But when he saw the wind, he was afraid and, beginning to sink, cried out, "Lord, save me!" Immediately Jesus reached out his hand and caught him. "You of little faith," he said, "why did you doubt?" (Matthew 14:29-31)

Peter walked on water. He moved towards Jesus. What happens, though, when he takes his eyes off Jesus? The wind and the roiling waves made him afraid, and he began to sink. He was walking on water, but when his gaze shifted from his Saviour to the dark and stormy circumstances, he began to sink.

Many commentators consider Peter an impetuous hothead, who regularly gets himself into trouble with his "speak first think later" approach to life. When I read this brief passage in Matthew, though, I see a lot of Peter in myself. Making audacious demands, stepping out tentatively in faith, and letting fear consume me. Perhaps you see some of those traits in yourself as well.

There is one word in those three short verses that moves me every single time I read them.

Immediately. Without hesitation, without pausing to see if Peter could right himself, without making Peter sort out his fear on his own. With powerful and tender love, Jesus *immediately* reaches out to catch him.

Where you look is where you'll land. If our miserable circumstances are all we can see, the wind and waves will frighten us, and we will sink. The words of Jehoshaphat come to mind again, "We do not know what to do, but our eyes are on you" (2 Chronicles 20:12). *Our eyes are on you, Lord. In the wild storm of life, when trouble assails and we feel beaten down on every side, our eyes are on you. When we can barely see through our tears, our eyes are on you. When we need perspective on the frailty of this life in comparison to your astonishing glory and majesty, our eyes are on you.*

Gaze on the beauty of the Lord, beloved. Remember, through glorious, restorative grace you may claim him as your own: your light, your salvation, your stronghold. The wild, brutal ugliness of this world will be a steady distraction, but fix your eyes on Jesus. Come to him, seek his face, and he will not fail to catch you.

COMPARISON

Psalm 73

Theodore Roosevelt once said, "Comparison is the thief of joy." It's a well-worn phrase by now, especially with women. When we fix our gaze on the green, green grass on the other side of the fence, we lose sight of the abundance right in front of us.

In the midst of trouble, it can be easy to see the lives of others and wish their goodness and ease was ours. Whether it's the put-together kids marching into church each Sunday or what feels like an endless stream of care-free vacations, the lives of others seem to shine brighter than ours, especially when our eyes are clouded by deep sorrow.

Comparison is an age-old problem. Asaph shares the same struggle as he opens Psalm 73: "They have no struggles; their bodies are healthy and strong. They are free from common human burdens; they are not plagued by human ills" (vv. 4-5). Asaph's sidelong glance at people outside of God's community leaves him comparing the hardship of his own life with the relative ease of theirs.

At times, we can reach the same conclusion Asaph leans

toward: *What's the point? Why am I living for Jesus when I am knee-deep in trouble and everyone else seems to be living a far better life?* "Surely in vain I have kept my heart pure and have washed my hands in innocence. All day long I have been afflicted, and every morning brings new punishments" (vv. 13-14). *What's the point?* The question arises in our hearts, doesn't it? Most likely, we do our best to keep it hidden, let our exhaustion and frustration alarm those around us.

Do you notice the echoing phrase at the end of verse 14? Perhaps the words "every morning brings new punishments" reminds you of the phrase we just looked at in Lamentations, where instead of punishment, we are assured of new morning mercies each day. The contrast is startling and evocative. We hold to the assurance of God and his mercy. Yet, when our gaze slips, our mornings look vastly different, and we experience punishment rather than mercy.

Asaph turns, then, and acknowledges the need for a corporate, eternal perspective. His gaze shifts off the seemingly delightful life of the wicked and returns to God, his assembly, and the protective mercy of eternal life. Matthew Henry beautifully articulates the conclusion Asaph reaches when he considers the final demise of the wicked:

> The righteous man's afflictions end in peace, therefore he is happy; the wicked man's enjoyments end in destruction, therefore he is miserable. The prosperity of the wicked is short and uncertain, slippery places. See what their prosperity is; it is but a vain show, it is only a corrupt imagination, *not substance, but a mere shadow*; it is as a dream, which may please us a little

while we are slumbering, yet even then it disturbs our repose (emphasis mine).[12]

Where we fix our gaze in the midst of sorrow matters, beloved. The temptation is strong to compare our challenging lives to those around us—whether we do so to gain perspective on our own pain or to nurse the pity gene we all carry. If, from the shadows of grief, we see only a shadow world of pleasure and delight, we risk missing the substance of the tangible goodness of God.

Comparison will rob us of joy without us even realizing it. In the shadows of grief and sorrow, joy may be difficult to find on a good day and compounding that with comparison will only make joy more elusive. Henry's eternal perspective (borrowed from the psalm) is not just an ethereal band-aid. True peace in the midst of ongoing grief or suffering is held quietly in the hands of what we believe of the future. If this bodily existence were the end of the story, truly our misery would be just that.

My husband, Len, has dealt with debilitating chronic pain for fifteen years now, and there are still those who want to talk to us about miraculous, bodily healing. Given the genetic basis for his pain, we consider this unlikely, from a human perspective. While we believe God is almighty and all-powerful, and most certainly capable of reversing Len's genetic makeup, we also know that the promise of healing in this life is not guaranteed anywhere in Scripture.

Does this mean we don't believe in healing? Absolutely not. We believe God promises healing and restoration to all his people, but we also acknowledge it may not happen on this side of grace. The assurance of restoration is still a balm for Len. As he keeps his gaze fixed on his Saviour, he is quietly confident that he will one day be restored. For as long as that healing is delayed on earth, there is grief and suffering, but also hope and certainty. He holds to the beautiful assurance of our eternal perspective promised through the life, death, resurrection, and ascension of Jesus.

When, like Asaph, your gaze shifts, and you see only the prosperity of the wicked, remember to cast a long glance at a far-off horizon, of a new heaven and a new earth. What we possess already, through the cross of Christ, is a foretaste of eternity, even amid the grief, pain, and loss. The promise of all our tomorrows is not a vague, wispy idea, but a solid, foundational promise. Cling to it when comparison robs you of your joy.

BROKENNESS

Psalm 73

During the dark days of infertility, the words of Psalm 73:26 were a sweet companion:

My flesh and my heart may fail;
But God is the strength of my heart
And my portion forever.

My flesh was failing me. Unable to conceive a child, I experienced a profound sense of bodily brokenness. What kind of woman can't do the one thing she was bodily designed to do? I watched women's bellies swell and grow new life within them. I couldn't help but stare at women pushing strollers and consoling toddlers. The comparison we looked at yesterday was slowly robbing me of my joy and leaving me thoroughly devastated. My physical inability to have a child was a deep, unrelenting grief.

The words of this verse are a statement of utter need. When everything is falling apart—when physical ailment or bodily brokenness occurs, when emotional pain and grief overwhelms and threatens to crumble everything we know and love—the psalmist knows the desperation of his need. He knows there must be more than this life in the valley of tears, and he claims his need with the same assurance as he claims the promises of God. Matthew Henry captures it this way: "The body will fail by sickness, age, and death; when the flesh fails, the conduct, courage, and comfort fail. But Christ Jesus, our Lord, offers to be all in all to every poor sinner, who renounces all other portions and confidences."[13]

Facing the possibility of never having children, I had to believe in something greater than myself. Even now, as we face a life without children (some 16 years later), the grief is no longer a raw, unrelenting pain. The grief lingers, sometimes surging in unexpected moments, but the pain has been eased by the joy of our life now and the confidence that we have a place and purpose in the kingdom of God, even without children.

My love of this verse remains: I need God. I need his mercies new each morning. I need the foot of the cross, where I can pour out my heart—both my needs and my sins. I need the transforming power of grace so I can love my neighbour. I need a daily reminder that apart from him, I can do nothing (John 15:5). I need the bright light of his joy, because joy apart from Jesus is a sputtering candle. I come before my God with empty hands and a broken heart, deserving nothing and receiving everything—more than everything, if that's even possible!

"But as for me, it is good to be near God." (Psalm 73:29) In this psalm, as in many others, a key distinction between the believer and the unbeliever is proximity to the presence of God. The NASB translates this verse as: "But as for me, the nearness of God is my good," which further illustrates the beauty of this idea. We have our ideas about what might be good for us, and, often, resistance to the idea of "other" good can create its own kind of suffering.

The word for "good" in this verse is a word that is used nearly 600 times in Scripture. It is the same root of the word God used during creation: "And God saw that it was good" (Genesis 1:31). It is also the same word used in deciding, "It is not good for man to be alone" (Genesis 2:18). It is the word Joseph used when reassuring his brothers in Egypt, "You intended to harm me, but God intended it for good to accomplish what is now being done, the saving of many lives" (Genesis 50:20). Our internal sense of what might be good for us is often not aligned with what God might find good for us. After all, our thoughts are not his thoughts, nor our ways his ways (Isaiah 55:8-9).

If we summarized this psalm in bullet points, it might look something like this:

- Surely God is good
- The apparent abundance of the wicked
- The inevitable demise of the wicked
- The abundance of knowing God
- The nearness of God is my good

The symmetry is poetic form at its best. Opening and closing with the goodness of God, and yet personalizing not only the outpouring of good we receive from God but also ascribing the goodness of God as *my* good. The apparent abundance of the wicked is worthless without the matchless wonder of God's presence. Their abundance is fleeting and temporary. In the brokenness of life, when our heart and our flesh are failing, God remains our portion. He is the portion that lasts and will not succumb to rot or mildew. "But store up for yourselves treasures in heaven, where moths and vermin do not destroy, and where thieves do not break in and steal. For where your treasure is, there your heart will be also." (Matthew 6:21)

COMMUNITY

Psalm 84

We were created for relational interdependence, and, most of the time, we hate it. Our innate tendency to push toward self-reliance and independence is a common pitfall, especially in an increasingly post-Christian culture. You can live your best life now, we are told. You can be better, do better, do more. Make sure your life is Instagram gold—tidy, beautiful, and exciting. Blend in a small amount of trouble or sorrow with the sometimes-insensitive comments of those around us, and we quickly convince ourselves we are better off on our own.

From the earliest pages of Scripture, God declared, "It is not good for man to be alone" (Genesis 2:18). The created order not only made man and woman in the image of God but also reflected the relational dependence of the Trinity. In the creation of Eve, "Adam goes from solitary to experiencing intimacy, union, community, fellowship, and love. But it is important to note that these relational virtues had existed eternally in the Trinity."[14]

We were created to need and depend on each other.

There will be those who insist that church attendance is unnecessary, and those who press hard that church attendance is a visual representation of faithfulness. Corporate worship, however, is also the avenue through which we are reminded how much we need each other.

Often, in grief, the reluctance to step through the doors of the church is powerful. We withdraw in pain and long to protect ourselves from either being swarmed by well-meaning parishioners or standing beneath a stream of comments we can barely stomach. In the midst of suffering, the question "How are you?" is one of the most hated questions by those in pain, since the sincerity of the asker is never certain. Do they want the whole truth? Are they committing real-time here in the buzz of the fellowship hall to hear the full story? Are they prepared to stand in silence as you share, holding respectful space for your story? Worst of all, are they just asking in the hopes of hearing you are doing well, better, best?

The beauty of the Psalms is their ability to capture the entirety of human experience in relation to the beauty of God. The inclusion of songs within the ancient psalter where the psalmist is longing to be in the house of God is a beautiful testament to our human need to commune with God in corporate worship. Psalm 42, for example, is a song of sorrow driven by the need to be in the house of God: "My soul thirsts for God, for the living God. When can I go and meet with God?" (v. 2). Absence from the body of Christ carries with it physical and emotional deficits: We hunger and thirst for the communion of those of the family of faith.

Psalm 84 paints a remarkable picture of the beauty of being within the church. The psalm is filled with imagery of inclusion and safety, of belonging and blessing: "Even the sparrow has found a home, and the swallow a nest for herself, where she may have her young—a place near your altar" (v. 3). The little, the least, and the lost have a place of safety within the house of God, for we belong in the presence of God and his people. We were created for this very purpose.

"Better is one day in your courts than a thousand elsewhere," the psalmist declares in verse 10, and our hearts soar. Spurgeon enthuses, "[If] Jehovah be our God, his house, his altars, his doorstep, all become precious to us."[15] We forget, sometimes, that the gathering of his people in his house is not the invention of man, but of God. It is God who designed the tabernacle and the temple and who set in place the rituals and liturgy found there. We may notice first the rules and regulations tradition may put in place, and we may pinch or squirm beneath them, but God is the origin and foundation of the body of Christ and those who dwell therein.

If your grief is holding you back from corporate worship, I understand. I have been there. With reluctant pain, we can acknowledge the church (in its overall abandonment of corporate lament) has not always fostered honesty and vulnerability as it might have. This can be a source of real and legitimate pain for those worshippers who are deep in the trenches of suffering and grief. If, for a time, you need to worship from afar, there is grace for this, too. There is grace for the moments where suffering and grief hold us back from encounters that may increase our sorrow.

With all gentleness and empathy, I quietly urge you not to let this last too long. The longer we worship apart from God's people, the more quickly our humble acknowledgment of the created order of our relationships will suffer. We were made for each other. I need the church, and the church needs me.

So perhaps you tuck yourself in the back and slip out quietly after the service. Maybe you ask a friend to sit with you to provide a buffer between you and the barrage of well-intentioned queries. If the swell of music causes tears to surge to the surface, perhaps you let them fall, regardless of who might notice. Here is an unfortunate truth: It may fall to the grieving, the chronically ill, and those who live with lingering suffering to reteach the church the necessity and importance of corporate lament. While we may not find ourselves strong enough to manage such a weighty task, be assured that walls are dismantled one brick at a time.

We were made for one another. You need the church, and the church needs you.

VALLEY
OF WEEPING

Psalm 84

O n Sunday mornings we probably drive a short way
to church. Perhaps we live close enough to walk,
and we move through the streets of our neighbourhood toward the building designated as church. Given
our modern proximity to both the physical building where
we worship and the various means we have to get there
quickly, the idea of pilgrimage is foreign to us.

Perhaps, from old church history lessons, you have vi-
sions of pilgrimage from the old stories—long, arduous jour-
neys to visit a certain teacher, shrine, or healing pool. Our
chronological distance from ancient Israel allows us to forget
the cultural and spiritual importance of pilgrimage. At least
once a year, families from throughout Israel would travel
(most likely on foot) to Jerusalem so that they could worship in the physical temple of God. As they traveled in large
groups (primarily for safety), the sound of their praise would
rise from them. The songs of ascents were written primarily

for these days of travel toward Jerusalem.

Psalm 84 also speaks of pilgrimage: "Blessed are those whose strength is in you, whose hearts are set on pilgrimage. As they pass through the Valley of Baka, they make it a place of springs" (v. 6). "Pilgrimage," in the original Hebrew, is actually a word better defined as "highways or course," a raised road whose primary destination is Zion. While Psalm 84 is not a psalm of ascent, it is suggested the reference here is broader and meant to explain a course of life: a life bent on seeking God's presence where it may be found.

This is further illustrated with some historical context:

The term "Zion" in the Old Testament is used as a kind of code word for the coming kingdom of God. Zion was a symbol of God's dominion over the whole earth, as well as the promise of a great future, when the Gentiles would come and submit to Israel's God. The worship at the temple was a foretaste of that future, when David's kingdom would extend over all humanity forever. The very presence of Zion in a human city, Jerusalem, was proof that God's covenant was with people and that, unlike the gods of the nations, he would indeed dwell among us.[16]

Zion was the promise of Immanuel: God with us. If the course of our lives is to seek the one who is already present, then our hearts are set on pilgrimage. Our lives are set on a course, a highway designed to lead us closer, step by step, to the presence of God. Ancient Israel may not have had the benefits we now possess in Christ Jesus—assurance of the constant, steadfast presence of God with us—but they understood what it meant to move steadily toward him. Their reference to Zion is a confident declaration of what God would bring about: a time when he would dwell among us—and not only that—that we would be indwelt by God himself, through the Holy Spirit.

Speaking of this pilgrimage, the sons of Korah are sure to include the Valley of Baka: the valley of weeping, or of tears. The valley of Baka is mentioned nowhere else in Scripture, and while historians and commentators are not entirely sure of the physical location, it is clear we are meant to understand one thing: We will walk through valleys of tears as we draw nearer to the presence of God. The Genenius Lexicon proposes an alternate understanding: "the valley of lamentations," suggesting that the actual location was likely gloomy and sterile.

Even when our hearts are set on God and seeking his constant presence in our lives, we may pass through the valley of lamentations, and it may not be too pretty. The landscape around us may look bleak and hopeless with dark cloudy skies threatening torrential rain. It may feel like a wasteland of sorrow and pain, and we may weep many tears, seeking rescue and relief. And yet, in the images of pools of water and autumnal rains, there is a promise of future restoration. For those whose hearts are set on God, the dark days are not the end of the story. We hold to the ultimate victory wrought by the blood of Jesus, and the promise of the renewal of all things. Grief may linger, but there will also be plentiful signs of life, the goodness of God, and brilliant hope for the future. As Charles Spurgeon says, "When we have God's ways in our hearts, and our heart in his ways, we are what and where we should be."[17]

TELL THE STORY

Psalm 107

The aural history of Israel is beautifully recorded in Scripture. Before the Bible was ever a book held in the hands of the literate, the redemptive history was bound up in the traditions of story-telling and remembrance.

According to the Israelites, forgetting God was less an accidental loss of memory and more an intentional, stubborn act of unlearning. While we consider forgetfulness as an annoyance or blunder, the ancient Israelite culture understood it as something significantly more.[18]

Over and over again, we read of memorials being set up so that Israel would remember what God had done and how God had delivered them. Ebenezer, for example, means, "Thus far the Lord has helped us," and it was represented by a tower of stones as a visual reminder for anyone passing by. (1 Samuel 7:12) When God instituted the Passover, he did so as a memorial of deliverance. The meal was created with this antiphonal question and answer designed to remind everyone present that God had delivered them out of Egypt (Exodus 12:26).

In today's psalm, we read, "Let the redeemed of the Lord tell their story—those he redeemed from the hand of the foe" (v. 2). Even with the written revelation of Scripture we can take advantage of today, it still falls to us to tell our story. As the redeemed of the Lord, we are to call to mind the questions and answers of our faith.

When Israel was called to recall the mighty works of the Lord, in order to be reassured of his faithfulness and promise-keeping, they did so in relation to the darkness from which they were delivered. Recalling the Passover would be pointless if they ignored the 400 years of slavery and brutality they endured in Egypt. Setting up Ebenezer in Mizpah would be irrelevant if Israel was not also meant to recall their near defeat at the hands of the Philistines.

Often, we want to smooth the rougher edges of the story to elevate triumph, when, in fact, we need to tell the story of both the darkness and the glory. When we tell the story of our grief—whether to a friend or the Lord—leaving out the black voids of pain and sorrow diminishes the astounding grace of God to reach us in our deepest grief. If we relegate our grief to a mere annoyance, we undermine the power of our story to glorify God's nearness and care. Imagine if we allowed ourselves to say, "I was sinking, and he didn't let me drown."

Psalm 107 walks us through some of the astonishing rescues and redemption wrought at the hand of the Lord. There are desert wastelands, utter darkness, prison experiences, bitter labour. The redeemed are telling stories of hunger, thirst, and affliction. They walked through tempests and storms only God could calm; there was nothing small or simple the redeemed suffered. And yet, throughout the psalm, as we read the accounts of pain, suffering, and sorrow, we hear again and again, "Let them give thanks to the Lord for his unfailing love and his wonderful deeds for mankind." (v. 8, 15, 21)

The magnificence of the Lord's deeds for mankind is held in close relation to the dire straits of his people. The psalmist has no fear about being direct about the extent of their troubles. As he tells the story, he is honest about the depth of affliction faced by the people of God, so that, by contrast, the saving work of almighty God would be showcased in divine power and compassion.

When we walk the shrouded road of sorrow, we can sometimes forget in the Hebrew understanding of it: a willful unlearning. When we struggle to believe God is near and good, we can find ourselves refusing to remember what we know to be true: He hasn't dropped us yet, and he has no intention of doing so.

The psalm closes with such a tender invitation: "Let the one who is wise heed these things and ponder the loving deeds of the Lord" (v. 43). It is a requirement of the human heart to place before our memories a constant reminder of the loving-kindness and abiding presence of our God. The Israelites raised many monuments in order to remember his wondrous works, and we are invited to do the same. The early church did the same, looking to the cross of Jesus and the perfect work that Love accomplished there. In the midst of our grief, we are wise to consider how we might raise up monuments of evidence of God's past and present faithfulness. As Matthew Henry writes, "It is of great use to us... to be fully assured of God's goodness."[19]

Tell your story, redeemed of the Lord. Do not whitewash or downplay the ugly parts of the story; declare them boldly. I could minimize my story by saying that I stubbed my toe, and it hurt a bit, but God was there. Or I could declare how utterly lost I was in my darkness, and yet, there in the dark, through the saving love of Jesus Christ, God was right beside me.

GOD WITH US

Psalm 139

When I first started writing about our infertility in 2005, I named my blog *Life as Two*. I considered it the height of cleverness, and I looked forward to changing the blog title to *Life as Three*, and then *Life as Four*, etc. It would be a fun, poignant chronicle of children joining our family. I was ridiculously proud of choosing that name.

Now, fifteen years out from that first blog post, the name remains with me. I never expected to still be living life as two. This was not the ending I had written for our infertility story. We are still childless, and while many days the awareness of that pulses quietly beneath the surface, there are some days where our life as two pinches hard.

Sometimes, we look back over difficult times in our lives and call the space of hard things a desert. A wilderness. It harkens us back, I think, to the people of God wandering in the desert, the painfully long process of reaching the promised land. The metaphor works for infertility, I think—the wilderness of childlessness, the promised land of parenthood.

If I think back on my journey, I can see those touchpoints.

If I narrow our story to that, however, does that mean I am still in the desert? Am I still wandering, awaiting a promised land? Or was the promised land only part of the purpose of the desert?

Let's step into Psalm 139 for a moment.

These verses also remind me of the desert wandering, the far and wide travel, the pillar of cloud by day, and the pillar of fire by night. God present with his people in the desert, guiding, protecting, leading. I sometimes wonder if the psalmist was thinking of the desert stories when he wrote this psalm. If he was looking back at the past faithful presence of God to reassure himself in the present.

If we try to self-define the promised land, we can get ourselves into some hot water. When I do so, I am often more fixated on the promised land (a child, for example) than I am on the presence of God. I want a reversal of circumstance rather than the God greater than my situation.

Consider Moses with me for a moment. Toward the end of Exodus, the Israelites have angered God yet again—this time with the building of the golden calf—and God urges Moses to take the people to the promised land. He will not go with them; God declares, for "I might destroy them on the way" (Exodus 33:3). Moses stands before God and replies, "If your Presence does not go with us, do not send us up from here" (Exodus 33:15). *Do not separate us from your Presence,* Moses pleads. *The promised land is no promised land apart from your Presence.*

The promised land can't be me with a child. It can't be

perfect, care-free circumstances. The promised land is no guarantee of non-stop joy or perpetual laughter. The metaphor only travels so far, of course, and perhaps I'm stretching it. God truly did promise his people physical land and a place he had chosen for them. Along the way, though, his presence was the constant in 40 years of wandering. The desert wandering is one of the earliest physical manifestations of Immanuel, God with us.

If your presence does not go with us, do not send us up from here.... God with us.

If I rise on the wings of the dawn and settle on the far side of the sea... God with us.

Jesus, born a baby, assuming our flesh and blood... God with us.

Here, in the desert, let us fix our eyes on Immanuel. The promised land is waiting, yes, but we don't know what it looks like. We can hope, we can pray, we can plan, but ultimately, the landscape of the promised land is a wide unknown. And yet, the promised land—just like the desert—is Immanuel. God with us.

PROTECTED

Psalm 16

When my father-in-law died in 2014, the Scripture at his funeral was taken from Psalm 16. As we gathered graveside to plant the seed of his body in the ground for the day of resurrection, the words of the psalm filtered through my mind: "...my body also will rest secure" (v. 9).

The wide plains of dusty grief can feel lonely, isolating. While we may share the same grief as family members, the cadence and tenor of our grief may not look the same. We may reach milestones within the phases of grief before or after others, and we can wonder if perhaps we are alone in our pain.

We can read a psalm like Psalm 16 amid pain and wonder if it true for us. We can question whether the "boundary lines have fallen in most pleasant places" (v. 6) and struggle to believe we haven't slipped from God's gaze. Finding this psalm tucked between other psalms of lament and sorrow, our temptation may be to slip past it and move on to something that better suits our mood.

John Calvin calls this psalm "a prayer in which David commits himself to the protection of God."[20] While he does not appear to be in distress in this psalm, there is a hum of need beneath the surface. In verse 5, David declares, "Lord, you alone are my portion and my cup; you make my lot secure." The confidence of his declaration is beautiful, and we may claim such confidence in our own prayers when we come before God.

If we look more closely at this verse and dig into the original Hebrew, we find a truly beautiful nugget of intimate care we may have otherwise missed. The original root of the word "secure" is *tamak*, which means to support and uphold. In modern English, we can infer all sorts of connotations for these words. Still, if we consider the meaning in the wider context of Scripture, we find ourselves in familiar territory.

In fact, we find ourselves on the hilltop at Rephidim. Joshua battles the Amalekites in the valley, and Moses holds his staff over his head to gain the victory for God and for the Israelite army. Beside Moses, we find Aaron and Hur, placing a seat beneath Moses's weary body and bracing his weakening arms with their own strength. The verb for Aaron and Hur's support is the same verb we find in our verse—an echo to a compelling visual where the support of the Lord can be interpreted as tangible leaning upon his strength when ours is failing.

So, too, do we see the raising of a wooden cross, rough-hewn and heavy. Upon it waged a battle only One could win, bearing the cup of God's wrath – meant for us – upon his very body. Bruised and nailed for us, Jesus made our lot secure. He eradicated a debt we could not pay to ensure our unlimited access to God almighty – his strength, support, love, and protection.

The Lord's protection over the whole of our life is not meant to be understood as an intangible, abstract idea. Scripture paints beautiful imagery of the lengths God will go to support us, of arms being lifted and braced by a power greater than our own. We can confidently declare to the Lord we need this from him and be assured of his faithfulness to provide.

The grace we witness in the light serves to declare God's mercy in the dark. A prayer for protection in moments of sorrow is as indicative of where our trust lies as it is when we are rejoicing at the majesty of Psalm 16.

When the cracks of our broken hearts are seeping with pain, we may remember this: God made our lot secure. Beneath us, he places a seat for our weary bodies, and he stands bracing our weakness in his power.

CARRY ME

Psalm 61

For a period of time, I lived with my sister and her husband. My nephew was a precocious toddler who loved going for walks around their country neighbourhood. We would wander over to the nearby school playground and ride the tractor. We would greet the animals in fenced fields along the road. On nearly every walk, he would turn to me, arms raised, and ask me to carry him. Usually we were close to home, and though I knew his legs weren't tired, I would scoop him up and he would wrap his arms around my neck and chatter the whole way home.

Carry me.

Spurgeon introduces Psalm 61 this way: "This psalm is a pearl. It is little but precious. To many a mourner, it has furnished utterance when the mind could not have devised speech for itself."[21] It has been readily established that we will find the parts of our own soul with the Psalms, and we see the truth of it. The honest portrayal of the troubled human heart and the plaintive cry for rescue to a trustworthy God is a repeated theme throughout Scripture. God is often more honest about our emotions than we are. He knows what we carry and how we fuss, not only because he created us but also because our flesh is held in heaven: our suffering Saviour who knew well the pain and exhaustion of living in these bodies.

> From the ends of the earth I call to you,
> I call as my heart grows faint;
> Lead me to the rock that is higher than I. (Psalm 61:2)

Carry me?

The evocative imagery of this psalm is wrapped both in the almighty saving power of God and in the tenderness of a heavenly Father. The original Hebrew for "heart" used here is the word *"ataph,"* meaning either heart (the seat of our emotions) or soul (our very being), but more than that, it carries a specific connotation: this is a soul wrapped in darkness. Calling from the ends of the earth evokes the idea that David feels far off from God and needs to call for God to hear him. It is a cry of desperation, as his weakness has overtaken him; he cannot climb himself to the safety of the rock. He needs help.

Carry me!

There is such a sense of settled assurance when a child is lifted into the arms of a parent. There is safety there—security, refuge, and rest. Tired legs can get a break. Intimate nearness can calm an overwhelmed heart and receive whispered reassurance. The child can rely on the strength of the parent to not only lift him but also to bear the weight of his needs.

When our hearts grow faint and God feels far away,

sometimes all we want is to crawl into the secure arms of our heavenly Father and burrow our face in his chest, sit cradled in the love of our Abba, and have a good cry. *Carry me,* we whisper.

There is a reason children want to be carried, especially if they are distressed or upset. Scientific research has shown that the mirror neuron system provides a renewed state of equilibrium when we are able to pick on non-verbal cues from those we love and who love us. Through the use of physical cues, including touch and body language, two people in a loving relationship can actually find their heartbeats slowing and matching one another. What a remarkable phenomenon our creator God has built into our neural network, further proving how deeply relationally dependent we are on each other.

Carry me…

> "Surely he took up our pain
> and bore our suffering,
> yet we considered him punished by God,
> stricken by him, and afflicted.
> But he was pierced for our transgressions,
> he was crushed for our iniquities;
> the punishment that brought us peace was on him,
> and by his wounds we are healed. (Isaiah 54:4-5)

He carried our pain and our suffering to the cross, punished on our behalf. He was pierced, stricken, crushed, and afflicted. He cried out in agony from the cross as the face of his Father turned away from him. By the wounds of the Holy

One we receive healing and peace. The body who carried his own cross paved a way for eternal access to the Father.

We serve the suffering Saviour, the Servant King who laid himself low for his chosen ones. When your heart is overwhelmed, may these opening verses of Psalm 61 remind you of the open arms of Christ Jesus. Reach for him, knowing he has purchased for you a peace only he could procure.

TASTE & SEE

Psalm 34

Our bodies were created with a sympathetic nervous system. In simple terms, this is referred to as "fight or flight", which regulates the body's response to dangerous or stressful situations. Heart rate quickens, blood pressure rises, and adrenaline courses through the body in response to a trigger of danger or stress. On the other side of the same coin, the parasympathetic nervous system works to restore equilibrium by lowering heart rate and blood pressure and returning the body to a renewed state of rest.

One of the ways the parasympathetic nervous system works to restore balance is through grounding exercises. Once, triggered by past trauma, my therapist walked me through something called the 54321 exercise, which is designed to counter to the body's response with trauma by grounding the mind firmly in the here and now. The 54321 exercise activates each of the senses, forcing the body to pay attention to five things it can see, four things it can feel, three things it can hear, two things it can smell, and one thing it can taste. As I focused on each of these things, taking deep breaths while doing so, my breathing slowed, my heart stopped pounding, and I was able to pull my mind away from past trauma to find a sense of equilibrium.

Our senses ground us to the here and now. It is a wondrous thing that God formed the human body with such intricate detail—detail scientists are still working to understand fully. It is no surprise, then, that Psalm 34:8 contains this beautiful phrase: "Taste and see that the Lord is good; Blessed is the one who takes refuge in him."

Taste and see. This isn't the first time in Scripture God uses the senses to direct us back to him. In the instructions to Moses for the tabernacle, included was a combination of plant extracts used to create an anointing oil reserved for the priests. A recipe of myrrh, cinnamon, calamus, and cassia, this fragrance was made sacred, and duplicating it for personal use was forbidden (Exodus 30:22-33). Scent is the sense tied most closely to memory, and God made sure that when this unique combination of fragrance would call to mind the tabernacle and his presence.

Perhaps it feels impossible to "taste and see" the goodness of the Lord. God is, after all, spirit, and we cannot reach out and touch him. Perhaps this idea feels too intangible. Let us look a few verses later, at the tangible response of God to his people:

> His eyes are always on us (v. 15)
> His ears are attentive to our cry (v. 15)
> He delivers us from trouble (v. 17)
> He is close to the brokenhearted (v. 18)

If this still feels too ethereal, think of Jesus. He turned water into wine. He touched the lame, sick, and blind. He rid the temple of the stench of greed and idolatry. He delighted in using visual imagery: the lilies of the field and the birds of the air, for instance. He multiplied bread and fish on the mountainside. He tasted the bloody sweat in the Garden of Gethsemane and the bitter gall of vinegar on the cross. In his resurrected body, he broke bread with his disciples on the shore of the sea.

The goodness of God is evident all around us, if we are willing to engage our senses to taste and see it. The lush green turning of spring, or the pure landscape of the first snowfall. The brush of a cool breeze on your neck, or the hot flow of a morning shower. The fragrant appeal of roses and dahlias and basil. The first bite of a sumptuous meal, or the thoughtful consumption of bread and wine at the Lord's table. When we train our senses as a guide to God's goodness, every aspect of our lives can come alive to his unavoidable goodness.

In times of sorrow, this is doubly true. Grief and suffering can set our sympathetic nervous system on edge; neurochemicals flood our brain and disrupt many aspects of life we typically take for granted. We struggle to envision a future from behind an opaque curtain. We find ourselves awash in guilt and sorrow over events and moments in our past. In days of trouble, sometimes we need to adopt a practice of grounding ourselves to remind ourselves God is near, present, and faithful and that "we lack no good thing."

FINDING REST

Psalm 62

G rief can be exhausting. Whether physical or ambiguous, loss can take up so much brain space. We can find ourselves having trouble sleeping, trouble eating, trouble pausing long enough to just take a deep breath and drop our shoulders. Let's do that now, for a moment. Let's just take a deep breath, and drop those shoulders. Maybe once more.

Rest is a rare commodity in our Western culture. We are a people who have learned to prize productivity and forward momentum above, well, almost everything. We want to present a polished, put-together appearance to the world. These markers are how we tend to signal to others that we are okay. Even though we may not be, there is an unwritten expectation that our grief has only a brief place among God's people. It can be equally exhausting to tie everything up in with a neat, tidy ribbon for the sake of others.

We bite back the tears in church on Sunday when the music moves our soul and emotions in the midst of our pain. We do our best to attend small groups, even though we can barely breathe. We struggle beneath our burdens, refusing to ask anyone to shoulder part of the weight for us.

Western culture's response to grief is often this: best to stay busy. Idle hands are dangerous. Keep working, and your brain won't have time to think about it. A week after my mother died, I was back in school, doing my very best to learn what a 10th-grade student is supposed to learn. It was determined that the best thing I could do was get back into a routine. Never mind the trauma of finding my mother dead on our couch, the soul-wrenching grief of burying her, or the overwhelm of moving into a new house with the kind and generous people who took my brother and me in. The best thing at the time, it was said, was for me to go back to school. Perhaps they were right.

Even as an adult, I catch myself prioritizing productivity over rest more times than I care to admit. I'm not villainizing work or its benefits, though I do wonder if, as a community, we have taught ourselves that God prizes our work over our rest.

Built directly into the creation order, God worked six days, and then he rested. I love how Crystal Stine, in her book *Holy Hustle*, summarizes this created order: "God worked and called it good, and he rested and called it holy" (177). It is significant that God ordains rest for the life of his people. Working hard has its value, but our human need for rest is so pressing God built it into the creation order. You will work, and that is good. And you will rest, for that is holy.

If rest carries such value, it begs the question: So what, exactly, qualifies as rest?

In verse 6 of Psalm 62, we find part of that answer:

"Yes, my soul, find rest in God;
my hope comes from him."

Let's take a quick look at the original Hebrew. The Hebrew word here is *"damam,"* and like many Hebrew words, it needs to be held in context to fully grasp the meaning. It can be translated as either "wait" or "rest," but the connotation behind it is stillness: to be silent before the Lord, patiently and with confidence to expect his aid. Do you notice how this rest is in no way passive? We aren't just lazing about on the couch, Netflix humming in the background. Rest is an act of intention. We hold ourselves still, and we do so in the confident belief God is for us. Rest is a willful act of quietness, submission, and assured hope.

The Hebrew word for "hope" in this psalm? *"Tikva"*. Literally, it means a cord. The very earliest use of this word in Scripture appears in the story of Rahab, who ties a scarlet cord in her window so the spies from Israel would know where she lived in the wall of Jericho. The scarlet cord was a sign of assurance for Rahab—that cord signaled her rescue and safety.

Hope is a scarlet cord of assurance, a line between God and us signaling rescue. If we can rest in stillness, confident of his aid, we are bound to him for rescue, refuge, and healing. Ultimately, in the life and ministry of Jesus, hope became a person—a scarlet cord to bind us in unity to Christ for all time. We can rest in this assurance today, friend. For he is gentle and humble in heart. His yoke is easy, his burden is light, and he will give you rest.

REST IN
HIS CHARACTER

Psalm 116

When I am having trouble sleeping, I often find myself singing the Genevan rendition of Psalm 116:

I love the Lord, the fount of life and grace
He heard my voice, my cry and supplication
Inclined his ear, gave grace and consolation
In life, in death, my heart will seek his face.[22]

One of the earliest psalms I learned to sing as a child, the words and melody return to me when I am restless and anxious. While quietly humming or silently recalling the words is no magic pill against insomnia, the Spirit uses the word of God to settle me again—to return me to my resting place: "Return to your rest, my soul, for the Lord has been good to you" (v. 7).

The original Hebrew for "rest" in this verse isn't referring to sleep or relaxation. The most accurate translation is a "condition or state of rest." The original word, *"manowach"*, occurs only nine times through the entirety of Scripture. Its first usage is in Genesis 8:9, when Noah sends out a dove toward the end of the flood to see if the waters have receded enough. The dove returns to Noah because it could not find a place to perch. Since the waters were still too high, the dove could find no resting place, no place to land.

This tangible expression of the noun allows us to envision what the psalmist is portraying here in verse seven: "Return to your rest." That is, find your safe perch, find your safe place to land. Do you have a resting place? I'm not talking about a favourite chair or vacation spot. I mean, in your heart of hearts, do you have an internal reset that quietly anchors you back to everything you know to be true about God? Perhaps it's a verse you've memorized that the Spirit recalls to your mind when your restlessness becomes overwhelming. In times of trouble, I have learned to return to this phrase: God is who he says he is.

There was a time, you see, when I did not truly understand who God was. Yes, I had been raised in the church, read the Bible at every mealtime, and sat beneath faithful preaching hundreds of times. I could repeat the correct phrases and responses when required, but, in my heart, I believed God was capricious and untrustworthy. Facing down dozens of platitudes by well-meaning brothers and sisters in the body of Christ in the face of losing my mother, I had drawn all the wrong conclusions in the anger and turmoil of my grief.

She's happy in heaven, so you should be too.

God must have needed her, so he called her home.

In my teenage mind, a God who needed my mother more than I did was a God I knew I couldn't trust. For years, this warped theology damaged me, building in me a defiant sense of self-reliance. If need meant you robbed people of what they needed, I would never ask for anything of anyone. For years, my writing was only a partially honest representation of my faith. Yes, I would share vulnerably (about infertility or grief), but I always made sure to tie everything up neatly with a ribbon, lest anyone find out the truth of my inner turmoil. I spoke the words of faith, but in my heart did not trust the God of that faith.

During a period of prolonged grief, as I watched my husband suffer beneath the weight of chronic pain and illness, my self-reliance began to crumble. I did my best to push through, slipping away from work at lunch to try to nap in my car. My doctor threatened to make me take a leave of absence from work, so I stopped showing up for appointments. At long last, through the loving pressure of friends who saw what was happening, I made an appointment and sat across from a counselor for the first time in years. Facing down my brokenness, my counselor sent me to the Psalms, with instructions to highlight every word that referred to God as safe and trustworthy.

I inched through the Psalms, and it was as if God had been waiting for me to open the Bible and read it honestly. As I turned the pages of Scripture, I could almost hear him whispering, *"Yes, beloved, I am right here."* Why it never occurred to me earlier to go back to Scripture to refute the idea that God needed my mother more than I did, I'll never know. On the pages of the Psalms, I found the answer I needed: I am who I say I am. You can trust me.

"Who do people say I am?" Jesus asked his disciples in Mark 8:29. Their answers were a mix of rumours and theories they had heard from various sources. Elijah, John the Baptist, one of the prophets... there was confusion and uncertainty, a shadow over their eyes and hearts to truly understand who Jesus was. "And who do you say I am?" Jesus presses his closest friends for their own confession. Peter steps in to reply, "You are the Messiah."

Those closest to Jesus could see who he was. Though perhaps their hearts marveled and wondered, they knew he was the Messiah, the long awaited Promise. The promise spoken in the Garden of Eden, now walking with them wrapped in humanity. Through the violence of the cross, Jesus sealed the truth of their confession.

When our hearts are flitting like a dove unable to find a branch upon which to perch, we may boldly answer the question Jesus posed to his disciples: *And who do you say I am?* God is who he says he is. Whether through tears, or in joy, or from beneath the sheets of my bed when I'm struggling to sleep, we know these words to be true: God is who he says he is.

We need only settle at the foot of the cross to know it is true.

THE
PROMISE OF PEACE

Psalm 85

"When peace like a river, attendeth my way,
When sorrows like sea billows roll;
Whatever my lot, Thou hast taught me to say

It is well, it is well, with my soul."

One of my favourite hymns, "It Is Well With My Soul," was written in 1873 by a man named Horatio Spafford. After a series of tragic events rival those found in the story of Job, the lyrics to this hymn were penned from a place of remarkable grief. The Great Chicago Fire of 1871 took the life of Spafford's four-year-old son, the economic downturn of 1873 ruined him financially, and, in 1873, the ship carrying his family to Europe sank. Though his wife survived, his four daughters were lost at sea. As Spafford crossed the Atlantic on his own to reunite with his wife, he composed the beautiful words of this familiar hymn.

We wonder how this happens. How, in the midst of

devastation and life-shattering grief, a man can pen words of such marvelous confidence. As the ship passed over the location where his daughters had drowned, how did a hymn land on his lips rather than a howl of agony?

"I will listen to what God the Lord says;
he promises peace to his people, his faithful servants"
(Psalm 85:8).

We often interpret peace as an absence of something else—conflict, war, noise. We made our peace, we say, when a relationship is reconciled. They signed a peace-treaty to close out a national conflict. We sink into luxurious layers of warmth and bubbles in the bath, reveling in the peace and quiet. Peace is the sweet sigh of relief when the skirmish is over.

The Hebrew word "*shalom*" is often translated as peace in our English Bibles. It is a word used over 200 times in Scripture, and, as is true of many Hebrew words, carries a broad range of connotative meanings. The general idea behind "*shalom*" is much less about a truce or cessation of conflict and much more about wholeness and harmony in relationship to God. According to Cornelius Plantinga, "In the Bible, shalom means universal flourishing, wholeness, and delight."[23] Peace, in Scripture, then, is far more than a stop to hostilities and violence. It is a spiritual state of wholeness rooted in the Gospel.

God promises peace to his people, and the lengths he was willing to go to accomplish that peace on our behalf should remain foremost in our minds. Jesus is called our

Prince of Peace (Isaiah 9:6) and assures us that the peace he gives us is not like the peace the world gives (John 14:27). And, of course, we have the verse that likely pops to mind from Philippians: "And the peace of God, which transcends all understanding, will guard your hearts and your minds in Christ Jesus" (Philippians 4:7).

There is no human understanding that can connect how Spafford could write such confident praise in a time of great sorrow. The very notion baffles us with its complexity and mystery. Can I stand in the pit of suffering and find peace? Can grief and joy share the same teardrop, the same breath?

"I will listen to what God the Lord says," the psalmist writes in verse 8, and here we are reminded that the peace of God transcends understanding. There are mysteries to the Christian faith we are not designed to handle. Our finite minds cannot grasp the full majesty of infinite God, and yet we are imbued with a peace we cannot explain. We come face to face with the mystery of being indwelt by the Holy Spirit and find ourselves confounded and bewildered.

"I will listen to what God the Lord says." And the Lord says, *"Shalom."* John Berridge captures this beautifully:

> But an upright heart will not be satisfied without hearing God speak peace to his heart by his Spirit. And for this he will pray, and wait, and hearken, and when God speaks peace, there comes such sweetness with it, and such discovery of his love, as lays a powerful influence on the soul not to turn again to folly. This peace is a humbling, melting peace, which brings humiliation to the soul as well as joy.[24]

We, too, as we ride the waves of grief, may confess with Spafford, "It is well with my soul." We listen to what God the Lord will speak—he who promises peace to his people—and in the humbling, mysterious peace, we find the answer we are seeking.

I am weak, but my soul is well. I am grieving, but I am held in peace. I long for healing, and I keep my eyes on Jesus.

"Whatever my lot, Thou hast taught me to say

It is well, it is well, with my soul."

GRIEF & JOY
HOLD HANDS

Psalm 90

The fourth book of the Psalms opens with lament.

Psalm 90 places the brokenness of the world—including human mortality—in the context of God's sovereignty. God remains in charge of all things, and our hope for the restoration of the broken to be put right rests solely in him. The brokenness of this world is evident in many aspects of our lives. Perhaps we have recently stood at the graveside, lowering the body of a dearly loved one into the cold ground. Perhaps we live with tattered relationships that show no hope of reconciliation. Perhaps we live daily with the loss of infertility, cycling through hope and disappointment month after month. Perhaps our bodies are riddled with disease and pain, reducing the shape and tenor of our days to something we no longer recognize. Our bodies, minds, and souls know we were not made for this pain and shadow. We were created and planted in a good garden, full of hope, promise, and intimate fellowship with God, and yet sin has destroyed everything it touches.

The lament we find in Psalm 90 is not a personal lament, but corporate. Its focus is on the pain of mortality as it relates to a sin-soaked world. Written by Moses, this psalm is an honest appeal to God for mercy.

> "You have set our iniquities before you,
> Our secret sins in the light of your presence"
> (Psalm 90:8).

As the leader of a stubborn people, Moses was well-acquainted with the effects of sin on this earth. Multiple times he had to intercede on behalf of the people, whether for their grumbling, their fear, or their defiant creation of a golden calf. Each time, Moses boldly stood before God to remind him of his faithfulness and the glory of his name. Not without his own sin, Moses acted outside of the commands of God, and it cost him access to the promised land, flowing with milk and honey.

As Christ-followers, we cling to the cross of Christ, knowing his perfect work of salvation completed for us what Moses could only hope for. While this does not change our need for daily repentance and honest, specific confession, there is a quiet tendency to gloss over the sin with a simple, "Forgive us our sin." Without naming our sins before a holy God, we can convince ourselves that perhaps God has not noticed them—maybe they aren't really that big of a deal.

God has set our iniquities before him, and our secret sins are not tucked away in the dark but set in full view in the light of his presence. Each sin he laid upon Jesus on the cross, pouring out the full weight of his wrath onto his only begotten Son. Who am I then to stand at the foot of that cross, lift my eyes to my tortured Saviour, and say, "This sin here? It's not a big deal."

True honesty with our utter need for Jesus is the hall-mark of wisdom. "Blessed are those who mourn," Jesus declared on the Sermon on the Mount—that is, blessed are those who understand they are spiritually bankrupt and nothing short of beggars. When we place our suffering in its true context—that this world is groaning for its restoration and that our suffering is inextricably tied to its brokenness—we can lament not only our pain and sorrow but also the true cause of it all. Therein we also find our hope, a promise we can count on: Christ is making all things new.

"In this life you will have trouble," Jesus told his disciples, "but take heart, for I have overcome the world!" (John 16:33). I wonder at times whether Jesus was thinking of this psalm when he said those words, for the sentiments of verses 14 and 15 resonate deeply:

> Satisfy us in the morning with your unfailing love,
> That we may sing for joy and be glad all our days.
> Make us glad for as many days as you have afflicted us,
> For as many years as we have seen trouble.

We want brief periods of trouble, followed by years of joy and ease. This is evident in how Christians in Western culture have adopted the phrase "a season of suffering." We have been told repeatedly in Scripture that we can anticipate hardship, grief, and pain for as long as our feet are planted on this earth, and yet, not only are we shocked when it comes our way, we hold our breath until it is over.

Grief and joy hold hands, beloved. "Make us glad for... as many years as we have seen trouble." In this life, we will face trouble—likely more often than we are interested in or prepared for. Yet also this: We may sing for joy and be glad all our days! These two do not cancel each other out; rather, they are intertwined by the complex mystery of faith.

The Christian perspective is a 360-degree perspective. We remember our created intention and the fall. We confess Jesus Christ and him crucified. We hold our present sufferings as the expected result of living on this side of eternity—not with glum resignation but with a heart of wisdom— while we experience the true joy found only in Jesus. And lastly, we look forward with immense hope, knowing that he who promised will come again.

"Jesus Christ is the same yesterday and today and forever." Hebrews 13:8

POSTSCRIPT
PRAYER

Lord God, I am crying out to you.
In the pain of my life, I am calling out to
the One who hears and answers.
You are my Creator, my Saviour, my refuge.
I praise you for the light you are in the darkness,
that Jesus is the light of the world.
Abba Father, there is so much pain right now.
I am weary of weeping, of prolonged sadness and grief.
Help me feel your presence, Lord God.
Remind me in big and small ways
that you are right beside me.
Carve into my sorrow-filled heart the
truth Immanuel – God with us.
When joy slips in to surprise, remind me
how grief and joy hold hands.
Let your peace – the peace that satisfies and
moves me toward wholeness – flood my
heart and draw me ever closer to you.
In Jesus name, Amen.

ACKNOWLEDGEMENTS

Writing is never a solitary task, nor is the life from which our words are drawn.

I owe Ben Nobels at Nobels Design Co a debt of gratitude for the beautiful cover art. You captured both the work and my heart behind it with precision and beauty.

Taryn Nergaard, for being a champion and also a layout pro. Thank you for taking this enormous task off my hands and doing it wondrously.

Kristin Vanderlip, for lending me your services in editing. I owe you at least a million dollars.

To Ian Wildeboer, for not only lending his name and his words to this book, but also for the use of his library. The access to the words of those wiser and more educated than myself is something for which I am exceedingly grateful. Thank you for also sharing your office as a quiet place to work during the weird and wild times of a global pandemic.

To Leslie Bartels, for being a Jesus-sister, encourager and prayer warrior. Our conversations always find me praising God for our friendship and our shared faith.

To Yen Gootjes, for being lovely in every way, and for lending me her studio for a day of writing. It was a cozy, delightful place to work, despite the rumbling of HVAC work in the building.

To my Sharkettes – Rachel Dixon, Esther Okerson and Dawn Torres. You are my cheerleaders, my sounding board, and my dearest friends. You have patiently endured my ramblings, rants, and fears over the past decade, and I am changed having known you. Thank you for the silliness, the honest vulnerability, the faithful prayers, and the safe place you are for me.

To Jennifer Geerts Brennan, for being a soul sister, beta reader, and all around beautiful friend. Thank you for being willing to hug me even though it's not your favourite.

To my Jesus family at Mercy Christian Church – your tender care of Len and me is a gift we cannot repay. Serving with each of you is a joy beyond measure.

To Small Group 2 – Corn & Mindy, Tim & Tree, Dan & Trish, and Jeremy & Lauren – I love you. Thank you for your faithful prayers, your willing vulnerability, and the oatmeal raisin cookies.

To my Saturday morning prayer group - Jazz, Jes, Lyndsey and Stacey - I love you, ladies. Thank you for drawing near to God with me early in the morning.

To my writing community, hope*writers. Y'all get me and this writing life, and it means the world.

To my two mastermind groups - you have opened my eyes to weird and wonderful ways of writing. To Katy Epling, Jazmin Frank, Eva Kubasiak, Taryn Nergaard, Cyndee Ownbey, Kristin Vanderlip, and Sara Ward - I joined this group on a whim, and you have embraced my work and set me on a wider journey than I could have imagined. Your prayers, feedback and critique are more valuable than you know.

To Jennifer Holmes and Tonya Salomons - you are my people. In all the ways, despite your shared hatred of mushrooms. Mushrooms are delicious, and an excellent source of potassium. Thank you for sharing space in this writing life, for your wisdom, encouragement, and grace.

To my father, Peter Blom, for living a life of quiet assurance in the midst of profound grief. Your honest faith has shaped mine in many ways, and I am deeply grateful for your care and wisdom.

Dawn Torres, I love your face. You are the iron that sharpens mine.

Len J, you are my whole heart and my best friend. Not a word of this book would have been written without your constant support and generosity. I know what it costs you when I take time away from the home-fires to write, and I will likely never be able to repay you. I'll spend my life trying, though.

And to my Lord and Saviour, Jesus Christ, apart from whom I can do nothing, may these words be an offering to lift and glorify your holy name. May my life and my words be a continual sacrifice of praise.

NOTES

1. "Parallel Classic Commentary on the Psalms", AMG
   Publishers, 2005

2. Tripp, Paul David, YouTube, Sermons, www.
   pauldavidtripp.com

3. Spurgeon, Charles, "The Treasury of David", Funk &
   Wagnalls, 1882

4. "Archaeological Study Bible: An Illustrated Walk
   Through Biblical History and Culture", Zondervan,
   2005, p. 820

5. Tyndale Old Testament Commentaries, Psalms 1-72 by
   Derek Kidner, Inter-Varsity Press, 2009

6. "Parallel Classic Commentary on the Psalms", AMG
   Publishers, 2005, p. 418

7. Keller, Tim, "How to Deal with Dark Times",
   YouTube, 2018

8. Henry Ford Health System, "How Coping with Grief
   can Affect Your Brain", 2018

9. Ibid.

10. Spurgeon, Charles, "The Treasury of David", Funk &
    Wagnalls, 1882

11. "Parallel Classic Commentary on the Psalms", AMG

Publishers, 2005, p. 127

12. "Parallel Classic Commentary on the Psalms", AMG Publishers, 2005

13. Ibid

14. Wegter, Jay, "The Holy Trinity and Social Relations", Gospel For Life, 2018

15. Spurgeon, Charles, "The Treasury of David", Funk & Wagnalls, 1882

16. "Archaeological Study Bible: An Illustrated Walk Through Biblical History and Culture", Zondervan, 2005, p.843

17. "Parallel Classic Commentary on the Psalms", AMG Publishers, 2005

18. "Archaeological Study Bible: An Illustrated Walk Through Biblical History and Culture", Zondervan, 2005, p. 843

19. Ibid. p. 543

20. Ibid.

21. Ibid

22. Anglo Genevan Psalter, "Book of Praise".

23. Plantinga, Cornelius, "Not the Way I t's Supposed to Be: A Breviary of Sin", 1996

24. Spurgeon, Charles, "The Treasury of David", Funk & Wagnalls, 1882

ABOUT THE AUTHOR

Thelma Nienhuis is a lover of Jesus, coffee, donuts & naps. She also loves words and people, and writes to remind you that grief is real, joy is possible, and God is near, faithful, and good. Amid suffering, we not only have permission to lament the dark, broken part of life, but also to be assured we live Immanuel: God with us.

Thelma has been writing about how grief and joy hold hands for over a decade, and you can find her writing on The Gospel Coalition, Fathom Mag, and (in)courage. She is also an occasional speaker and podcast guest, sharing about infertility, grief, and spousal caregiving.

When she is not writing, you can find Thelma holding the couch down, surrounded by snuggly dogs. Thelma lives in Hamilton, Ontario, with her husband, Len.

@thelmanienhuis

www.thelmanienhuis.com

Made in the USA
Columbia, SC
18 December 2020